PRAISE FOR
EXIT FOR MILLIONS

"The cold hard fact is most business owners will never sell their business. One day, they'll simply shut the door, turn off the lights, and fade out. What a shame. Nick Bradley has the formula business owners need to turn their company into a sellable asset, something that brings life-changing wealth. If you're serious about cashing in on what you've built, read this book now, before the door closes on you."

—MIKE MICHALOWICZ, **Author of *Profit First* and *The Money Habit***

"Entrepreneurs on fire! If you're building a business with the dream of a lucrative exit, *Exit For Millions* is your roadmap. Nick Bradley delivers actionable strategies that align perfectly with the principles of financial freedom and fulfilment. This isn't just a book; it's a call to action for those ready to take control of their entrepreneurial journey. Prepare to IGNITE!"

—JOHN LEE DUMAS, **Host of Entrepreneurs on Fire**

"Most entrepreneurs chase growth but forget the endgame. *Exit For Millions* gives you the blueprint to scale and sell—on your terms. Nick Bradley shows you how to build with the exit in mind from day one. Read this if you want a company that's not just growing, but worth buying."

—CAMERON HEROLD, Founder COO Alliance,
Author of *The Second In Command*

"You sold the business. You're on the beach. Now what? Nick answers the question nobody talks about—what happens after the deal, when the money's in and the identity's gone. (Besides just being rich.)"

—JAMES SCHRAMKO, Author of *Work Less, Make More*

"If you're building a business to serve others and create freedom for yourself, then *Exit For Millions* must be your next read. Nick doesn't just teach exit strategies—he teaches how to build a business that lasts, attracts the right customers, and lets you walk away proud. This book feels like a mentor in your corner."

—PAT FLYNN, Author of *Lean Learning, Will It Fly?* and *Superfans*

"*Exit For Millions* gives entrepreneurs a clear, real-world playbook for scaling with purpose and exiting for serious upside. As an operator and private equity expert, Nick brings a rare perspective from both sides of the deal table. This is essential reading if you want to exit on your terms and use that success to create real freedom."

—JUSTIN DONALD, #1 *WSJ* and *USA Today* Best-Selling Author of
***The Lifestyle Investor*, Founder of The Lifestyle Investor**
Mastermind, Host of *The Lifestyle Investor Podcast*

"I've always marvelled at how many business owners leave money on the table when selling their business because they don't know the path to follow to maximize their exit. Nick Bradley's process lays out the roadmap from scaling to selling and all you have to do is follow it. He makes it simple to make millions, what more could you want?"

—TREY TAYLOR, Managing Director, Threadneedle, the Taylor Family Office

"Nick Bradley's *Exit For Millions* resonates deeply with the principles of purposeful scaling. He demystifies the exit process, providing entrepreneurs with the tools to not only grow their businesses but to do so in a way that reflects their core values and long-term vision. This book is an essential companion for any leader committed to meaningful growth."

—BRENDAN MCGURGAN, Co-Founder and Author of *Simple Scaling*

"No successful business owner would ever launch a new product without understanding their clients and the problem they are solving. And yet business owners start businesses all the time with no idea who the eventual buyers will be or how to build the business to deliver the best value and get the best price. In this book, Nick shows you exactly what you need to do to tweak your strategy to get the optimum rewards for your years of hard labour. What could have been a dull manual is instead infused from start to finish with Nick's engaging personality, great storytelling, and genuine desire to help business owners avoid the many pitfalls out there. When the poacher turns gamekeeper, you listen to where the traps are hidden!"

—CALLUM LAING, Entrepreneur & Investor, Author of *Boardroom Blueprint 3* Other Best-Selling Business Books.

"I have exited my own business that was doing eight figures, and I wish Nick had written this book ten years ago… Large strategic buyers and private equity firms play four-dimensional chess, and the typical private business owner often plays checkers. This book is a playbook on how to play the game at the level necessary to go into the Superbowl of your entrepreneurial career to make everything you've risked owning and running a company worth it!"

—RYAN TANSOM, **Founder, Arkona**

"Nick Bradley has created an invaluable resource for anyone looking to grow and exit their business the right way! *Exit For Millions* contains real world wisdom and practical advice taught by a true expert in the field of buying and selling businesses. If you are looking for a practical, no-nonsense guide to selling your business, I highly recommend *Exit For Millions*!"

—MATT ANDREWS, **CEO, Family Mastermind**

"In *Exit For Millions*, Nick Bradley delivers a masterclass on building and exiting a business with integrity. This book is essential for any leader committed to creating lasting value and making a meaningful impact."

—KEN ESLICK, **President of The Leaders Lab**

"Nick Bradley is a pioneer in the world of helping entrepreneurs navigate the landscape of growth, equity and understanding the world of business. As a doctor this book made exiting a business simple yet attainable for any entrepreneur regardless of their past experiences! Five stars for *Exit for Millions!*"

—DR. ALOK TRIVEDI, **aka Dr. Rewire, Author of *Chasing Success* and *Wired for Wealth***

"*Exit for Millions* hit different for me. I've scaled multiple companies, but this was the first time I felt like someone truly laid out how buyers think, what they're looking for, what makes them pay more, and what gets overlooked. Nick doesn't speak in theory; he gives you the real playbook. If you're serious about building a company that someone actually wants to buy for a premium, this isn't optional reading... it's required."

—ROHAN SHETH, **CEO, GrowRev**

"I've been alongside Nick in the trenches and seen him use this private equity playbook to create extraordinary value growth. I was also there when he made the decision to share it with the world through his award-winning podcast, *Scale Up with Nick Bradley*. This book is the natural next step. A must-read for any entrepreneur serious about building a valuable business."

—ROB J WILLIAMS, **Fielding Global**

EXIT FOR MILLIONS

ALSO BY NICK BRADLEY

PODCAST

Apple

Spotify

EXIT FOR MILLIONS

THE **PRIVATE EQUITY BLUEPRINT** FOR SCALING & SELLING YOUR BUSINESS FOR MAXIMUM VALUE

NICK BRADLEY

FOREWORD BY **CARL ALLEN**

FIELDING HOUSE PRESS UK

FIELDING
HOUSE
PRESS UK

Published by Fielding House Press UK
Wansford, United Kingdom

The information provided in this book is for informational purposes only and is not intended to be a source of advice or credit analysis with respect to the material presented. The information and/or documents contained in this book do not constitute legal or financial advice and should never be used without first consulting with a financial professional to determine what may be best for your individual needs.

The publisher and the author do not make any guarantee or other promise as to any results that may be obtained from using the content of this book. You should never make any investment decision without first consulting with your own financial advisor and conducting your own research and due diligence. To the maximum extent permitted by law, the publisher and the author disclaim any and all liability in the event any information, commentary, analysis, opinions, advice and/or recommendations contained in this book prove to be inaccurate, incomplete or unreliable, or result in any investment or other losses.

Content contained or made available through this book is not intended to and does not constitute legal advice or investment advice and no attorney-client relationship is formed. The publisher and the author are providing this book and its contents on an "as is" basis. Your use of the information in this book is at your own risk.

For information about special discounts for bulk purchases or author interviews, appearances, and speaking engagements please scan this QR code to contact us:

First Edition

ISBN hardcover:	978-1-0682439-0-5
ISBN softcover:	978-1-0682439-1-2
ISBN ebook:	978-1-0682439-2-9
ISBN audio book:	978-1-0682439-3-6

Development, book design, production by Rodney Miles, www.RodneyMiles.com
Edited by Marc Concklin, www.ConkCreative.com
Proofread by Anne Concklin, www.AKCEditing.com
Cover design by Greg Merrilees, www.Studio1Design.com

Note to Readers

Before We Begin: A Note on Professional Advice

Exit For Millions is based on my experience advising and investing in businesses, leading exits, and working closely with private equity firms. The strategies, insights, and frameworks in this book come from real-world application across multiple sectors and deal types. But let's be clear: this book in itself is not a substitute for getting professional advice.

Scaling and exiting a business successfully requires expertise across a wide range of areas: legal, financial, tax, compliance, accounting, and more. That expertise must be specific to your business and your jurisdiction. So, as you move forward, I strongly encourage you to seek out and engage qualified professionals who understand your context and can give you tailored, fact-based guidance.

This book is not designed to provide legal, tax, or financial advice, nor does it promise a particular outcome. It's here to give you the mindset, models, and tools that have worked for me time and again in helping business owners build scalable companies and sell them for maximum value ... but like anything, individual results can vary.

Think of *Exit For Millions* as your strategic blueprint—a way to approach your business with the same mindset, rigour, and systems as a private equity investor. My aim is to help you see the bigger picture, avoid costly mistakes, and unlock the value you've built—on your terms.

With the disclaimer out of the way, let's get started!

"Entrepreneurs think they make serious money running a business. The truth is, you only build life-changing wealth *scaling and selling* one."

—Nick Bradley

DEDICATION

*To my wife Carrie, and our girls, Arabella and Matilda—
Thank you for your love, patience, and unwavering support
while I wrote this book. I am endlessly proud of you, and I love you with
all my heart. You remind me every day why the journey matters.*

*I make reference to my dad a lot in this book as he was the catalyst that
sparked my personal transformation. But it was my mum, and my
grandparents, that taught me courage, purpose, and provided me with the
best foundation. I'm forever grateful for that.*

CONTENTS

FOREWORD

BY CARL ALLEN

OVER THE PAST thirty years, I've played the high-stakes game of mergers and acquisitions, completing more than 330 deals totalling over $48 billion in value. In that time, I've worked alongside global industry titans, helped countless entrepreneurs transform their businesses, and built Dealmaker Wealth Society into a powerful resource for those looking to scale, sell, and achieve genuine financial freedom.

But here's something you learn fast in the dealmaking world: The real secrets — the ones that genuinely move the needle and separate average entrepreneurs from legendary successes — are rarely found in textbooks or business school classrooms. They reside behind closed doors, guarded closely by insiders, institutional investors, and elite private equity firms.

Enter my friend Nick Bradley, and his extraordinary new book, *Exit for Millions*. Nick has finally cracked open those doors, providing entrepreneurs unprecedented access to the exact strategies, tools, and tactics the world's most successful private equity investors use to scale, structure, and ultimately sell businesses for maximum value.

This isn't theory. This isn't guesswork. Nick Bradley has lived it, personally overseeing more than $5 billion in successful exits and sharing his knowledge with entrepreneurs globally through his acclaimed *Scale Up* podcast — which boasts over a million downloads in 130 countries. And let me tell you, having been in this game for decades, Nick is the real deal. Reading this book feels exactly like sitting across from him — getting direct, actionable advice from a trusted advisor who's been deep in the trenches.

What impresses me most about *Exit for Millions* is that Nick didn't hold back. Every chapter is packed with precisely the kind of pragmatic, immediately applicable guidance entrepreneurs desperately need. Whether you're looking to exit in the next year, the next five years, or you're simply seeking the tools to scale a self-sustaining business that provides ongoing financial independence, this book gives you clarity, confidence, and — perhaps most importantly — control over your entrepreneurial destiny.

The truth is, great businesses aren't built by accident—and neither are successful exits. Every deal I've ever closed came down to having the right strategies, the right people, and the right insights at the exact right time. This is precisely what Nick Bradley delivers with *Exit for Millions*.

This book challenges you not only to think bigger but also to act bigger — to move beyond simply running a good business and step into the world of extraordinary results. Nick's insights give you the tools to avoid the costly mistakes, wasted opportunities, and painful regrets I've seen far too often in my career. More importantly, he empowers you to secure the kind of exit most entrepreneurs can only dream about.

So, if you're ready to take control of your entrepreneurial journey — whether you plan to exit for millions, scale sustainably, or simply ensure your business works for you rather than the other way around — you're holding the exact blueprint you need. This isn't just another business book; it's your competitive edge in the biggest deal you'll ever make.

Dive in, embrace these insights, and let Nick Bradley guide you to the life-changing exit you've earned.

Carl Allen

Founder, Dealmaker Wealth Society
Investor, Entrepreneur, and M&A Expert

INTRODUCTION

I WAS JOLTED awake at 3:00 a.m. by an excruciating pain in my face. My entire jaw throbbed, as if I'd been bitten by something. I bolted to the bathroom and stared in the mirror at a man who looked like he'd been punched in the face with knuckle dusters. Terrified, I checked the inside of my mouth and found little shards of *something*. But what?

Apparently, I'd crushed down on my jaw so tightly that I had fractured two molars. In other words, I was so stressed out that my body had decided to shatter a few teeth while I was asleep just to get my attention. Now I found myself asking the man in the mirror: "How did you get here?"

The answer was clear: I'd gotten there by experiencing extreme stress in both my personal and professional lives.

On the professional side, I had been working in *private equity*[1] (PE) for many years. I had scaled and exited businesses in the most cutthroat corner of the financial world, closing deals in the billions while learning the secrets of selling to sophisticated investors. With over 50 acquisitions and 27 businesses sold, I had played a pivotal role in creating over $5 billion in value. But I was also living in a constant state of fear of who I was becoming, and I had zero regard for the value created by the people whose businesses we relentlessly took over.

On the personal side, I had reunited with my father, who left my family when I was only two years old. He had emailed me years before around my 40th birthday stating that he wanted to re-enter my life, and I'd decided that I owed it to my younger self to hear what he had to say. As we talked in a pub for the first time in decades, I couldn't stop the tears from rolling. Everyone had told me that my dad wasn't a nice guy, that he left us because he didn't love us enough to stay. As I listened to *his* side of the story, though, I learned that he used to be a successful entrepreneur, possibly even a millionaire before he was 40. He lost his first business in a terrorist attack in Melbourne, Australia, but he had started another one and built himself up again.

Over the next few years, I learned that the entrepreneurial spark I'd felt since my teenage years was more "genetic" than I'd realised. More importantly, I learned that my dad was now genuinely a nice guy.

Then five years after he sent that first email, Dad told me he'd been diagnosed with cancer.

All of this ran through my head as I stared back at the man in the mirror. As my personal and professional stresses joined forces, a haunting realisation washed over me: Those founders and entrepreneurs we'd been taking advantage of all those years in my PE life were more than numbers on a spreadsheet. They were flesh-and-blood people *just like my dad.* My dad, who spent decades of his life recovering everything he'd lost. Who wasn't around when I was younger, and now regretted not seeing me grow up. And who was now fighting an even scarier battle with cancer — a battle he would eventually lose within twelve months of his diagnosis.

After returning from the dentist to have my broken teeth fixed the next morning, I had a long chat with my wife. "I want to make a change," I said. "The stress of private equity is affecting me physically. I hate who I'm becoming. I don't want to be this cold, disconnected, ultra-competitive person who's not fun to be around. I want to be a better husband, better father, and better role model for our kids."

My wife smiled. She could tell I meant what I was saying. She knew I needed to make a change as much as I did. Maybe more.

After that conversation, I called up a friend from university. We thought he was a bit odd back in the day because he was always into mindset and personal development, and he never used to go out drinking with us. No surprise, he became a millionaire before he turned 30. After hearing my situation, he said, "Get yourself to a Tony Robbins event, and be open-minded about what you learn."

I saw an event coming up in Chicago. So in June of 2018, I jumped on a plane and spent four days listening to Tony Robbins. At one point, he flashed a quote on the giant screen:

> "You will get all you want in life, if you help enough other people get what they want."[2]
>
> —Zig Ziglar[3]

As I stared at those words, my entire belief system changed. I realized that my life to that point had been about my own significance, all about me. Now I understood the truth: *If I can help others, I don't need to be fearful about getting everything for myself anymore. It will just come through that act.*

By the end of the conference, I made the decision to shift from my side of the private equity table to the other side. I took one last PE job to smooth the transition, but I also launched a podcast to tell my story and start building my personal brand. The podcast shot to number one in the U.K. business charts and stayed there for weeks. After a year, I left that last, unfulfilling PE job. And I've been doing my own thing ever since.

To be clear, I've never seen private equity as inherently "bad." It lives on the cutting edge of business, and it can teach you the best practices for establishing, scaling, and exiting a company. I just knew I could no longer be on the exploitive side of it. I needed to switch teams and work for those extraordinary business owners, like my father.

Since then, I've dedicated my life to helping entrepreneurs grow, scale, and exit their companies on their own terms. To achieve freedom and help them reach the next, best chapter of their lives.

This book is a huge part of that.

It's too late to help my own father. But I know in my heart that it's never too late to help *you* — the founders out there struggling just like Dad did. Luckily, two decades of scaling companies with intense precision has given me a unique ability to diagnose issues, implement solutions and create value for struggling businesses.

I've translated that deep understanding into the Scale To Sale™ Methodology revealed in this book. Because the cold, hard truth is this: The biggest marketplace for high-value exits is private equity. Nearly 10,000 private equity firms[4] exist in the world today, and in North America alone, these firms have over $4 trillion — yes, *trillion* with a "t" — in "uninvested funds[5]." All that money is sitting around waiting to be spent, yet over 70% of businesses listed for sale never find a buyer. And of the ones that do, many sell for far less than they're actually worth.

That's a tragedy, especially when you've poured your heart and soul into building your business.

I don't want you to miss the opportunity of a lifetime. That's why I'm playing for *your* team now: so you can level the playing field with the PE Sharks. I'm going to take you inside their secret world, expose their hardball tactics, and prepare you to go toe-to-toe with them. Ultimately, I want you to walk away from your most valuable asset richer than you ever thought possible — in more ways than one. Because as I've learned first-hand, "value" is about more than money.

Bottom line: Selling your business doesn't have to be a game of chance. With the right guidance, strategy, and support, you can navigate every complexity, scale efficiently, and achieve an exit that truly reflects your life's work.

This book is for you if:

- You're thinking of selling your business in the next 1 to 5 years, and you don't want to fall prey to sophisticated buyers such as PE firms.

- You're excited about retiring or reinventing yourself, but you're nervous about screwing up and missing the opportunity to set you and your family up for generations.

- You want to know the traps that PE Sharks set for business owners like you, and how they can snare you into believing that subpar offers are your *only* option.

- You're willing to face hard challenges and the hard decisions to achieve a high-value exit.

Does this sound like you? Then let's begin this amazing journey.

LEAVING THE MATRIX

> "You take the blue pill, the story ends. You wake up in your bed and believe whatever you want to believe. You take the red pill, you stay in Wonderland and I show you how deep the rabbit hole goes."
>
> —Morpheus in the film *The Matrix*

In the film *The Matrix*, Morpheus presents Neo with a choice: Take the red pill and step outside the Matrix, or take the blue pill and stay inside the illusion. In other words, remain ignorant and in your comfort zone, or learn the truth.

In my own life, I've been presented with that choice time and time again. After a lot of trial and error, I've learned to choose the red pill every time. I took the red pill to transform from a fat kid into a personal trainer (and even a professional model for a brief time). I've aggressively climbed multiple corporate ladders. And I made a lucrative living hunting businesses for more than a decade. I was one of those sharks in the world of private equity using every legal trick in the book to give my firm[6] the upper hand. If you know the TV show *Billions* on Showtime, I was Bobby Axelrod. I would have looked at you from across the table and thought, *I'm going to totally and utterly destroy you.*

That is, until I took the red pill that led me to write this book.

As I climbed one corporate ladder after another, I struggled with internal battles. I was becoming ultra-competitive, aggressive, and not very pleasant to be around. Then I experienced my breaking point. One day, my boss came to me and said, "Nick, I want you to do something, and you're not going to like it. But I'm gonna pay you a truckload of money if you get it done."

He wanted me to be part of a team that would make over 500 people redundant (that's "laid off" for my American readers) all in one go. I would have walked over anybody to get to my next promotion or bonus, so I said "yes" without batting an eyelash. Even worse, I didn't find it difficult to fire all those people. I had become so unemotional, detached and self-focused that I saw those redundancies as simple, tough decisions that any good businessperson has to make.

One firing in particular stands out, and I'm certainly not proud of it. After listening to my corporate jargon, a man whose life I'd just upended looked at me and said, "I hope you enjoy your blood money." I planned to, but the joke was on me. When the job was done, I asked my boss for the bonus he promised. "Guess what?" he said. "I'm not gonna pay you."

This sparked one of the biggest red-pill/blue-pill decisions of my life: *Do I get out of this company, or do I stay and watch myself turn into the wealthy, powerful, egotistical, narcissistic alpha male (my boss) standing in front of me?*

I took the red pill, and I took off.

That led me to work for Getty Images[7] in London and New York, where I was properly introduced to the world of private equity. Getty was owned by a firm that raised private investments from high-net-worth individuals, endowments, and pension funds. Those investments were used to acquire and scale those companies, usually through a complete takeover called a *buy-and-build*, or *rollup*[8]. The firm would then sell the full group for stupendous amounts of money — I'm talking in the *billions*.

I spent three years at Getty doing multiple deals, then the next seven in the elite world of private equity. I helped PE firms acquire these undervalued businesses, scale them up or turn them around, and ultimately sell them for a killing. I had to make all sorts of difficult decisions along the way — including letting people go — and this made me even more unemotional and detached. At the core of it, I wanted to win solely on my terms and timeline.

My external battles were nothing compared to my internal ones. Working with big numbers and huge amounts of money made me feel sick, because I knew deep down that I wasn't doing what I was meant to do.

Partly as a coping mechanism, I started running marathons. I've now completed over 60 marathons, including 24 ultra-marathons, but I did most of them when I was going through the pain of pretending to be someone, I wasn't in the crazy PE environment. Like an alcoholic or drug addict, I did it to desensitize myself and escape. I still love to run, but back then I did it to stay alive. I was so compulsive that I would get up on a Sunday morning and run an entire marathon just for training.

Luckily, as I stated in the Introduction, I took another red pill to escape this unsustainable situation. I made the key, life-affirming decision to help business owners instead of taking advantage of them for the benefit of a private equity firm. Today, I'm living my dreams. I spend more time with my family. I speak professionally. My podcast now has over a million downloads that have impacted businesses in 130 countries. And I've written this book. I'm proud to say that I've never been happier.

But enough about me. Let's talk about *you.* If you're like my clients, you're successful, somewhat wealthy and respected. But it's time to experience the other fruits of your efforts. Maybe it's time to enjoy some freedom and start the next chapter of life — all those things you had in mind when you started out. This book maps the path to realizing *all* your dreams through a beautifully executed high-value exit. And it starts with learning the tactics perfected by private equity.

Why don't all business owners grow their businesses according to the *secret playbook* of private equity? Usually, it's a lack of money and/or knowledge. But with expert guidance, you can enjoy all you ever hoped for when you went into business, and maybe even a lot more.

Many business owners spend all their time building a great business, but they don't know how to get the proper reward as they transition. Imagine standing on the precipice of the most significant decision of your life. You've poured your heart and soul into building your business, and now you're considering an exit. But your expertise is in *starting* and *growing* a business — *your* business. You probably aren't an expert in *selling* a business, and you don't know the tricks that sophisticated buyers use to minimize your business's value.

Having sat on the other side of the PE table, I can tell you that it all comes down to one question:

Is PE going to see you as the prize or the prey?

The difference between those two words is the difference between walking away from the closing table with your head held high or having the bitter taste of regret in your mouth for the rest of your life.

When your business is viewed as the "prize," you'll walk into the negotiating room radiating confidence. You won't actually *need* to sell your business, but you'll do it for the right price. You're in a great position to negotiate.

When you're viewed as the "prey," you'll appear unsure and apprehensive. The PE Sharks will smell your fear. They'll know they can get your business for a bargain, and they'll pounce. In the end, you'll be so beaten down that you might actually *thank* them for basically stealing your business as they celebrate over an expensive dinner and a bottle of rare Scotch. On you, of course.

But here's the good news: You can still choose your fate. You can be the prey, or you can be the prize. You can get taken, or you can secure the future you've worked so hard to achieve.

With the tactics you'll learn in this book, I assure you that you'll be the prize, and you'll be unstoppable. The PE Sharks will see you as a peer, not a victim. You'll be viewed as a shrewd business owner who knows your value and expects what's rightfully yours. PE buyers will fall over themselves trying to acquire your company.

How will you know you're there? When you can answer *yes* to each of these foundational questions:

- Are my systems and processes well-documented, allowing me to run my business like a well-oiled machine that'll make buyers compete to take over my business?
- Are my financials strong, showing consistent growth year-over-year?
- Is my business on an upward growth trend, setting me apart from my competitors?
- Is my team strong, committed and capable of driving my business to success without me at the helm?

You're probably not there yet. Few businesses are. Most are a diamond in the rough, with great potential but lacking the polish to shine. That's fine, so long as you have the guts to challenge your current ways of thinking.

I share my personal and professional journeys in this book not only because they explain why I wrote it, but because I know how hard it is to sell a business for its true worth. Thinking it'll "simply happen" is blue pill thinking. Choosing the red pill is harder, but more rewarding. You have to zig when everyone else zags. Get outside your comfort zone. And make the difficult decisions.

I started my first business when I was 18, and I sold it for $3,000 Australian. The last business I was involved in sold for over $2 billion at a very large *multiple*.[9] I've been where you are, and I wrote this book for you. Because you deserve the value you've spent your life building.

It starts with taking the red pill. That's what I did after experiencing crushing stress and reconnecting with my dad, only to have cancer take him away again. I'm going to keep taking the red pill, and I want you to make the same commitment.

WHAT IS A "HIGH-VALUE EXIT"?

Maybe you've taken your business as far as you can. You don't have the energy you used to, and it's time to move on. In that case, private equity is the best resource in the world for scaling your business into something even more extraordinary. It's *your* best option for achieving a high-value exit.

We'll discuss several exit options in this book, but three main options apply to founders, CEOs and entrepreneurs:

1. You no longer run the day-to-day operations of the business. You bring in a new CEO, and maybe you join your company's Board of Directors.

2. You leave altogether, perhaps even the Board. You retain some degree of ownership, but you no longer exercise governance and are simply an investor.

3. You actually sell your shares in the company and fully exit ownership.

So, what constitutes a "high-value exit?" I define it as scaling and selling your business successfully for an amount of money that will change your life. It's about fully realising *your* number vs. selling your company for less and being taken advantage of by sophisticated buyers. Your life-changing number is personal, of course, and we'll discuss more about that concept in Part 3, Step 1 of the Scale to Sale™ Methodology.

If you remember one thing from this book, it should be this: Selling your business is like selling a house. If you put it on the market "as is," you won't generate as much interest. It won't appeal to the right people, and potential buyers will leverage inspection reports to demand price reductions.

How do you get the most money for your house? You make repairs and renovations before putting it on the market. You fix the foundation. You paint the rooms. You improve the landscaping. You stage it for your target buyer so they can see *themselves* living in it instead of you. Your house becomes the prize that buyers compete to win. You generate a bidding war, and instead of leaving money on the table, you sell it for over the asking price.

The same principles apply to selling a company. Yours might be making money "as is," but the difference between a business that's exitable and one that isn't is *how well it can transfer to someone else*. If you're building a business just for revenue, profit and income, you're only playing half the game. If you want to sell one for millions or billions, you must treat it like extremely valuable real estate and stoke a bidding war among potential buyers.

A PE Shark coming into your business wants to work out if you're a worthy adversary — the prize or the prey. They hope you *don't* know the secrets I'm about to reveal in this book, because then you're the prey, and they can take advantage of you.

Unfortunately for them, I'm about to translate my PE and investor-backed environment experience into a step-by-step guide to making a high-value exit. In other words, your future sophisticated buyers have no idea what they're in for: They're about to give you the life-changing, high-value exit you deserve, because you're going to be the prize.

WHAT THIS BOOK IS & ISN'T

I'm not here to teach you how to grow your business one customer at a time. Books like that focus on sales and marketing, and frankly, they're a dime a dozen. This book is about teaching you a better and faster way to *scale your business before selling it for its highest valuation.*

It's often said that if you want to become a millionaire, do real estate. But if you want to become a billionaire, do *mergers and acquisitions*[10] (M&A). That's essentially what this book is about. Ninety percent of all millionaires got their wealth by investing in real estate[11], but only 7% of all billionaires got there the same way[12]. The other 93% largely got there through M&A, which is the heartbeat of private equity. M&A and PE are so completely complementary, they're like the left and right hand of wealth creation.

I'm about to take you into the secret world of private equity and teach you my proven Scale To Sale™ Methodology. I guarantee it'll change the way you think about your business. You'll be able to stop wasting time and money on ineffective growth strategies. Instead, you'll be able to build an "exitable" business regardless of your industry, or whether you want to sell right now or not.

We're going to do this in three parts:

- **Part One:** What are the 15 characteristics of a high-value business?
- **Part Two:** How does the secret world of private equity operate, and why is it important to know?
- **Part Three:** What does my Scale To Sale™ Methodology involve, and how can you apply it to *your* business?

Before you turn the next page, know this: *The number one reason businesses like yours don't sell is that their owners haven't envisioned their next act in life.* That's right, getting cold feet kills the deal. I've seen many owners get paralyzed mid-process because they never imagined their life outside their business. The result: They miss out on the opportunity of a lifetime.

This book is about making a lot of money for your hard work, but it's also about feeling self-esteem, pride, recognition and excitement about your future — and quite possibly even creating generational wealth.

For me, it's about my dad. He wasn't perfect, but there's a lot of him in me, and I don't want to make the same mistakes he did. Ultimately, I want to look at myself in the mirror and — instead of seeing a swollen jaw — see a person who's proud of who he is and what he's becoming. I want to know with full commitment that I'm helping business owners like you get the value you deserve for what you've created.

Let's get started.

KEY TAKEAWAYS

- Over 70% of businesses listed for sale never find a buyer.
- Sophisticated buyers are trained to snare business owners into accepting subpar offers or terms by making it look like their only option.
- "Stress" is really "fear."
- Most business owners know how to build a great business. They don't know how to sell one.
- You have to take the red pill to be successful. Assuming that selling your business will "simply happen" is blue pill thinking.
- When you eventually sit across the table from the Private Equity Sharks, you'll want them to see you as the prize, not the prey.
- Selling a business is like selling a house. Selling "as is" limits your value. A high-value exit means fixing what's broken — repairing, renovating, and staging your "property" to generate maximum demand *before* you put it on the market.

PART ONE

A High-Value Business

You Don't Build Real Wealth Running a Business. You Build It Selling One.

HAVING YOUR OWN business is a great first step to achieving everything you hope for in this life. The time demand can be staggering, but business owners enjoy an autonomy envied by nearly everyone else.

But here's the thing: Not every business owner will build enough wealth in their lifetime to achieve freedom with enough time to enjoy it — even if they make decent money (which they often don't). Maybe this describes you: You work around the clock chasing leads and trying to grow a business that *could* generate wealth and freedom, only to see the same sad fact in every annual financial review: You're not building your business in a way that will eventually deliver the freedom you've always dreamed of.

We're not going to make that mistake, because I'm going to help you do three things:

1. build a high-value business,
2. reach a life-changing capital event,
3. and unlock your personal freedom.

If you feel trapped in the very business you created, don't lose hope. You're not necessarily doing anything wrong. If you've gone from start-up to scale-up, then you obviously know how to run a business. You simply need to align your growth strategy with your bigger life ambitions and discover the highest-value way of *exiting* your business on your terms and timeline. And that's why you're here.

Start by asking yourself a simple question:

Do I currently have a high-value business?

Let's find out

15 Characteristics of a High-Value Business

[Free Download] The Exit For Millions Blueprint™

If you could start a business over from scratch, you'd build it to be sellable in the future — even if you never intended to sell it. This mindset sets the stage for a powerful exit one day (if you choose it) and provides a framework for holistic growth and success.

If you didn't start your business with selling it in mind, don't worry! Selling a business is like selling a house, and you still have time to give your current business/property the "curb appeal" and deep value it needs to attract buyers. Along the way, you'll also reduce your headaches and stop missing opportunities, so it's a win-win.

I've identified 15 factors that give a business the scrumptious chum it needs to lure the hungry PE Sharks. Keep in mind that PE is unapologetically about money. Selling your business for lots of it is a game, and there are rules. You may not like them, but you have to know them to win.

As we do this, score your business. Who knows, you might have 10 of these 15 factors already in place, so you might be close to being able to sell your company to private equity already. If you have all 15, you could probably take your business to market today. But if you only have one or two, which is completely normal, then you have work to do.

#1: YOU HAVE STRONG CASH FLOW

Does your business generate huge amounts of EBITDA[13]? No one, especially private equity, wants to buy a business that isn't growing and cash flowing. "Future value" drives the *multiple*[14] the PE Sharks are willing to pay, so you need a sustainable growth story — a plan that drives growth and generates cash into the future.

But the business is worth this amount today, you might think. That might be true, but when someone agrees to buy your company at 10–15 times your average EBITDA, they expect it to grow for the next 5–10 years or more. Getting a 10x on your EBITDA is the same as getting paid 10 years' worth of profit *in a day*. No one's going to fork that kind of money over if you haven't built a stunning company with a powerful growth story.

#2: YOU HAVE A UNIQUE & DIFFERENTIATED BRAND

Is your brand unique, or is it swimming in a "sea of same"?

By "brand," I don't mean the colours of your logo, the distinctiveness of your font or the quirkiness of your reception area carpet. I mean the entire positioning of your business. The products and services you sell. The way you deliver them. How your people show up. In short, your entire reputation.

A unique and remarkable brand is *differentiated.* Think Apple or Nike. Their brands stand for (and against) something. People seek them out because they're different. They have cachet. When your brand has that, it's often a license to print money.

If your business is perceived as generic, it's in a *commoditized market.* You can't compete on service or value, so you have to compete on price. The brand that can lower prices the most and remain profitable wins. That's a *race to the bottom*, and it's not a market you want to be in.

#3: You Have a Highly Capable Leadership or Management Team

Are you still running most of your company's operations? That's a problem. It means your business depends on you, and private equity doesn't like that.

I've seen businesses with strong financials — high eight-figure revenues, maybe eight figures in profit — with owners or founders who are deeply ingrained in their operations and customer relationships. Translation: too much risk. Their business can't be sold, because what happens when that founder suddenly has millions in their bank account and loses interest?

I only buy companies when I'm confident the owner isn't going to take his or her payday and ride off into the sunset or has built a team that's capable of running the show if they're not around. If the business will fall apart the second they leave, then it's not a high-value, transferable asset.

#4: You Have Recognized Talent Across Your Organization

Do some of your key business roles lie outside the C-suite[15], leadership team or board? Case in point: Getty Images had a small team responsible for integrating acquisitions. They were extremely tight, competent, experienced and well-structured, but their leader didn't sit on the board. If I were mapping Getty and looking at it from a private equity standpoint, my observation would be, *There's strong talent in a key area, in key roles, aligned to the business strategy.*

When you're looking at your own business, you need to think the same way. A great leadership team is key, but you also need great specialists across your entire organisation to maximise your valuation.

#5: You Have a Well-Defined Performance Culture

By "culture," I mean behaviours — how you hire, fire, incentivize, etc. The starting point of culture is *values*, which are the operating model of how you influence performance and do things in your business.

If your people are delivering on business goals, but doing so in a bad way (say, unethically), then private equity isn't going to buy. You might have great numbers. But if everyone in the business is an ass, or your culture is considered "toxic," that's going to affect your value.

Uber[16], WeWork[17], Enron[18] — all these supposedly "successful" businesses suffered from massive cultural issues, and their valuations plummeted the minute the press learned about them.

Culture is as important as strategy, and you need to weave them together. If you haven't worked on values in your business, an easy starting point is Gino Wickman's book, *Traction.* Gino shares some valuable thoughts on how you can set up values in your business and hold yourself accountable to them. It's a great starting point for entrepreneurial-led organisations, and I've used it often.

#6: YOUR MARKETING, SALES & DELIVERY DON'T RELY ON YOU

Are you still handling all of your sales and marketing? Are you the literal face of your business, and do you personally own your key customer relationships? Then good luck selling your business.

Similar to #3 (leadership) and #4 (talent), to attract the PE Sharks, you need to build a machine that's transferable. As you scale, you need to bring in people *who are better than you* at the business's core competencies:

- acquiring customers (marketing),
- selling them something (sales),
- and delivering (fulfilment).

Many owners and founders fail to create a high-value company because their egos get in the way, or they're simply control freaks who are afraid to let go and trust others.

In short: If you want them to fork over the cash, then hand over the reins.

#7: YOU HAVE MULTIPLE CUSTOMER ACQUISITION CHANNELS

Do you have one primary lead source that works predictably? Great. But do you have a backup plan if it fails? If you don't, your business could go backwards overnight, and PE doesn't like that.

When I talk about having "multiple customer acquisition channels," I mean having several ways to drive opportunities into your business. By "predictability," I mean knowing that if you do certain things, you're going to get a result. For example, if you spend x amount on Facebook ads, you're going to get y number of leads.

If PE looks at a company that doesn't know how it's going to generate its next piece of business, then it knows it will likely have to do the additional marketing work itself. That's not a risk, per se, but PE isn't going to give you any value for it. In fact, they're going to devalue your business. If, on the other hand, that function is already working well (or you can fix it on your own), then they're going to pay more for your business.

You want at least 2–3 customer acquisition channels. And you need to measure their performance so you're always optimising, improving and then scaling what works efficiently.

#8: YOU HAVE A PREDICTABLE, LOW-CHURN[19] BUSINESS MODEL

"More than half your marketing time should be devoted to your existing customers."

—Jay Conrad Levinson[20]

Are you constantly hunting for your next customer, then finding that they only buy *once* from you? Bad news: You're not running a high-value business. The PE Sharks want you to bring customers in, sell them one thing, then then sell them another thing, and eventually move them into a subscription model or other long-term relationship. Why? Because that creates strong *lifetime value*[21].

PE loves this because it means you're getting huge efficiencies from your marketing. You're finding a customer and increasing their average order value (getting them to buy more from you in a single transaction) and measuring what they spend with you over time.

Put simply, private equity loves two things: *recurring revenue* and *lifetime value*. Recurring revenue means that someone purchases in a predictable way. Lifetime value means they do that over a long period of time. If you have a predictable way of bringing people in — and they buy reliably for one, two, or three years — then congratulations! You have a "predictable, low-churn business model."

Do I look at the standard "cost-per-lead" when valuing a company? Sure, but it's only part of the picture. Consider this quote:

> "The business that can outspend its competitors on advertising always wins."
>
> —Unknown

That sentence has always stayed with me. Here's what it means:

Say you have a relatively high cost-per-lead compared to a competitor. Maybe they spend $10 per lead while you spend $50. On the surface, that looks bad. But what if your back end is so good that every time you snag a lead, you monetize it in multiple ways? And what if the competitor who can only afford to spend $10 per lead can't compete with your ability to spend $50 per lead? They can't win new business effectively from that advertising channel, and they often can't compete at all. Meanwhile, you can make your money back 10 times over, which means you're *sweating the asset*[22] of what you've already secured. If that's the case, then your business model is based on lifetime value, and you're going to win every time.

This is why SaaS[23] companies have traditionally earned such high valuations. Once a customer comes in, these companies embed them into subscription models, and they don't leave. That's *low churn*. If you have it, private equity loves you.

#9: YOU HAVE A DIVERSE CUSTOMER BASE

Do you rely on only a few customers to generate most of your revenue? That's called "concentration risk." Say 2–3 customers supply 80% of your revenue. If two of those customers suddenly leave, then revenue drops 50–60%. Guess what the PE Sharks think of that?

High-value businesses spread their revenue across multiple customers and customer segments. At Getty Images, we had four major divisions:

1. **Media:** This included content shared with global news channels, as well as access to some of the largest sports and entertainment brands (NBA, NFL, Academy Awards).
2. **Agencies:** Long-term contracts with the world's biggest agency groups.
3. **Corporate:** Many of the *Fortune 500.*
4. **Unassigned small businesses**: This was the *long tail*[24], and it was my area. Because we had a digital platform and small businesses bought content from us, I could take the same content we sold to big businesses and make it accessible to smaller ones. Many customers hardly bought anything, but it still added up to hundreds of millions in revenue.

That's a highly diversified set of channels, and we had different models against them. When we sold Getty to private equity, we had diversification across all of them. If the media channel underperformed because the market changed, then we could upgrade our activity with corporate or agencies, or vice versa.

If you only have one channel in your business, with one or two customers driving most of your revenue, then private equity won't see you as "high-value." Diversify ASAP.

#10: Your Systems & Processes Are Fully Documented

If someone stepped in to run your business tomorrow, would they have an instruction manual to work from? They should.

I previously mentioned the importance of having *people* in key roles to run your business without you. The same applies to *processes*. Your business needs to be structured to run when you're not around or if some of your leadership team members plan to leave when the business is sold. That means documenting every key process to establish SOP (standard operating procedures); creating key role profiles; knowing how handoffs between marketing, sales, fulfilment, etc. should work; and looking at systems that will make jobs easier and more efficient. Having a solid person overseeing operations (CEO) or other operations leader is essential, but it's even more important to have a good operation overall.

Entrepreneur James Caan said it best. He's on the hit U.K. television show *Dragon's Den* (think *Shark Tank* in the U.S.), and when an interviewer asked him about the importance of people vs. process, he said, "Watch this." He called someone on his phone, and a man soon walked in and handed him a document. James explained (emphasis added):

> "This is his entire job manual. Everything that man does in this business is in there. This document manages him, so I don't have to. They have to know I'm watching, but they don't need me to manage them. If he leaves, I can hire someone else who can follow this document and do the job well. **I don't like to rely on people, I like to rely on processes.**"[25]

#11: YOU'RE HITTING YOUR KPIS[26]

Do you measure the key things in your business that drive performance? These are your KPIs, or Key Performance Indicators. If you don't have anything in place and don't use technology to track these metrics in real time, then the PE Sharks will find a different food source.

Private equity craves precision, data and insights, so it loves businesses that are run by performance metrics. If you don't know your financials, leads, fulfilment, churn or employee engagement, then you don't have the instruments to fly the plane. That means you expect a new owner to jump into the cockpit without charts, controls, or gauges.

Private equity demands metrics. Without them, they won't be able to evolve, pivot, and drive the right strategies to earn the right results. Before you consider selling your company, make sure you already have them.

#12: YOUR FINANCIALS ARE AUDIT-READY

Are your financials ready to be reviewed by a third party *right now*? If you'd have to leaf through mountains of paperwork and gigabytes of spreadsheets to find them, then you're not audit-ready from the PE perspective.

Too often, I go into a business that thinks it's doing well because it measures basic revenues and costs. That's not nearly enough for private equity. They want *quality of earnings* (sometimes called "Q of E"[27]), which is a far more sophisticated measurement.

Yes, about 60% of your company's value to private equity will come from your *people*, *processes*, *structures*, *brand* and *culture*. We'll talk more about these elements later in this book. But that still leaves nearly half of your valuation to bottom-line financials. If you don't already have a top-notch finance team, hire a CFO, finance manager or *fractional finance*[28] *team*. The great ones are out there, and they'll help you achieve audit-readiness.

#13: YOU HAVE A HIGH-QUALITY BOARD OR ADVISORY TEAM

Could you prove to a PE Shark *today* that your business benefits from excellent corporate governance? Let's hope so, because the first thing they're going to do when they buy your company is put a management board over you and assign an *operating partner*. I know this because I used to be one.

Some PE firms will give the operating partner position to a Harvard MBA with a strong financial brain, and you're going to have some governance. But the more you can demonstrate how well your business operates *before* that, the better. Because it lowers — here's that word again — *risk*.

If you own a free-spirited, entrepreneurial company, a PE Shark is going to think, "How will these people react when I install a board that values structure and discipline?" If he or she concludes that the culture — and thus, the business — might fail, then no deal or a lower valuation. If, however, you can demonstrate that you have strong guidance and a coachable leadership team, then PE will place a higher value on your business.

#14: YOUR EBITDA IS AT LEAST $5 MILLION

Did that number scare you? Don't worry about it, just get there.

Many of you reading this book may not be able to check this box yet, but *$5 million plus* of *EBITDA* (sometimes called "net profit") per year is a magic number. Why $5 million instead of $3 million or $4 million? It's just a fact. Private equity will sometimes buy businesses that fall short of this number, but if you want to create certainty, then you need to get to $5 million.

Buying a big business may seem to present a bigger challenge vs. buying a small one. But the private equity principles I work with often say some version of this:

> "I don't want to muck around with a small business. I want to buy something bigger, because if I can bolt that EBITDA onto what I'm already doing, then I'm going to get to my end game quicker. And my end game is getting at least 3–4 times return on my investment capital."

If you currently sit at $1 million EBITDA, you can get to $5 million pretty quickly. If you're at $3 million EBITDA, you might be able to sell your business now, but you're probably going to be bolted onto another business that's already been acquired by PE. You can still get a good multiple. But if you want to be a *platform*[29] — the first purchase in a given market by a specific PE firm — and then do a *buy-and-build*[30] strategy with them, then $5 million EBITDA[31] is the absolute minimum from my personal experience.

When I work with founders and companies who want to scale to exit, I like to set a $5 million EBITDA target. And it's a fun ride to get there! Of course, if you're already at $5 million+, then why not go for a $10 million EBITDA target and sell your company for over $100 million? It's possible once you know how to play the PE game.

#15: YOU'RE READY TO SCALE STRATEGICALLY

Even if your business isn't growing quickly today, is it at least positioned to scale via mergers and acquisitions (M&A)?

The private equity playbook is based on *acquisitions*. PE isn't just going to buy *your* company. They're going to buy other businesses, bolt them together and sell the group to a bigger PE firm (or possibly a larger corporation, or even launch an IPO). Conversely, they might buy you and bolt you onto something else. Either way, if your foundations aren't strong enough to grow by M&A, then PE is going to see you as lower value.

The more you can show that you've built your company through acquisitions — that you've bought at least one entity in the past — the more attractive you're going to be. PE loves owners who can prove that M&A isn't a new concept to them. So, when they buy you, they won't have to teach you a whole new way of growing your company under their guidance.

Based on my real-world experience in the private equity world, these are the 15 characteristics of a high-value business that attract PE interest. How did you score? If you didn't check many boxes, don't worry. The rest of this book is about how to get there.

Keep in mind: At the time of this writing private equity coffers held about $4 trillion in unspent investments. Their investors aren't getting a return on that money *and* they're paying management fees to the PE firms. PE firms *want* to invest. Their investors *want* them to invest. If your business is small and underperforming, then you only have a 20% chance of attracting their attention. But if your annual revenues are over eight figures and your business has strong EBITDA, then you raise your chances to about 80%.

Let's continue our journey to your high-value exit by sneaking you into the secret world of the PE Sharks. Trust me, they don't want you to know what I'm about to tell you. Because the more you learn about how they operate, the better you'll do when negotiating with them. Quite possibly, you'll even win the game.

KEY TAKEAWAYS

- Most business owners don't build enough wealth in their lifetimes to achieve absolute freedom in time to enjoy it.
- You don't make serious money running a business, only selling a business. And the biggest marketplace of buyers for your business is private equity.
- Building your business to attract sophisticated buyers like private equity brings tremendous benefits, even if you never intend to sell.
- Creating a PE-friendly business comes down to optimising 15 characteristics. If you don't already have all 15 (and virtually no business does), the Scale To Sale™ Methodology is designed to get you there.

PART TWO

The Secret World of Private Equity

Your Invitation & Initiation

THINK OF THE private equity world as an elite club in London or New York — the kind where members pay an obscene amount of money to join. "Regular people" don't know about these clubs. They're invitation-only, and there's no sign on the door. Inside, the PE Sharks smoke cigars and drink thousand-dollar bottles of wine as they share war stories and compare strategies to win the game vs. small business owners.

I'm going to bring you into one of these clubs — we'll call it Club Hammerhead — and sit you at a table with a group of PE Sharks. They're going to assume that you're one of them, so they're going to speak freely — not knowing that you're filing away everything they're saying to use against them.

First, let's find out who these people are and what kind of world they live in.

EXAMPLE #1: GREAT WHITE CAPITAL

In a nutshell, here's how private equity firms operate:

1. They raise funds from investors.
2. Those investors expect the PE firms to invest their money through mergers and acquisitions (M&A), buying businesses and bolting groups of companies together through a process called *rolling up*[32].
3. The PE firms sell those bundles for three to four (or more) times the *total amount of money deployed* to create the roll-up. (Sometimes the PE firms will go back to investors and leverage more of the fund to execute their strategy, plus adding any required debt to the deals.)

Here's a very simple example to explain how this can work:

Five high-net-worth individuals each pitch in $10 million to create a *private equity fund* called Great White Capital.

5 investors x $10M = $50M creates Great White Capital fund

Great White eyes its first company — its "*platform*" — which is worth $40 million but will require another $10 million in improvements. Great White makes this investment, but only using about 20%-30% (let's say 25% for our example) from investor money. The rest comes from secured debt, with the business being acquired as the collateral.

First "platform" purchase = $50M

($40M purchase + $10M improvements)

Investor funds $12.5M (25% of $50M)

+ $37.5M secured debt against the business

Great White then improves and builds the platform company's value through various techniques. I'll get to those soon, but one of the most common is acquiring another company — maybe even two or three. Say Great White Capital does that, then its members pitch in to buy another $50 million business (again, with a mix of investor money and debt). They know that this will effectively raise the value of the platform business over the next few years.

Great White now has a group of companies it has collectively acquired for $100 million.

It oversees the growth of its acquired platform (the two businesses combined), with the goal of raising its value by three or four times the initial invested capital — typically in three to seven years. If you do the math, that means Great White is gunning for a $300M–$400M valuation for its group of companies within the specified timeframe. Once Great White achieves that goal, it can sell the businesses and split the earnings.

For our first example in this book, and to keep things simple, that's $40M–$60M profit for each investor, plus the return of their initial $5M.

The investors committed $10M each to the fund, $50M in total, but only $25M was called in total or $5M each. The fund bought the platform company for $50M but only used $12.5M of capital with the rest debt-financed ($37.5M) so each investor would be asked to contribute $2.5M.

They then do another purchase for the same price ($50M, again using $12.5M of capital, meaning each investor would face a capital call of $2.5M), making the total called capital for each investor $5M. *It's only when there is a capital call that an investor's money transfers from their bank account to the fund.*

So, $100M has been invested in a combination of debt and capital. When they arrive at the targeted valuation of $300M to $400M, that will be either a *3X MOIC or 4X MOIC (multiple on invested capital).*

But it gets even better than that, because Great White pays back the debt over the life of owning the group of businesses — using the company's profits to pay back this debt — thus, their individual returns are actually much higher!33

See why private equity creates so many millionaires and billionaires? No other business or asset class can produce that much

ROI in such a short time. Learning this *before* you sell your business is an absolute game-changer.

If this example leaves you a bit confused, no worries. We'll run a few more in the coming pages.

THE GROWTH OF PRIVATE EQUITY

With more and more people discovering the power of private equity, its model has grown wildly in recent decades. Consider these facts:

> "In 1980, there were 24 PE funds; in 2015, there were roughly 6,600 PE funds; and by 2022, the number of PE funds had soared to more than 19,000. Perhaps more astounding is the growth in total *assets under management*[34] (AUM). In 2000, PE firms in the aggregate held $579 billion in AUM. By 2022, that figure had surged to about $7.8 trillion."
>
> (https://content.naic.org/cipr-topics/private-equity)

> "Private equity AUM (assets under management) has continued to grow at a steady pace, and we expect it to reach $7.6tn (trillion) by 2027 despite macroeconomic headwinds, a substantial leap from 2021's $4.2tn."
>
> (https://www.preqin.com/insights/global-reports/2023-private-equity)

"According to a recent report from Ernst & Young LLP (EY) and the American Investment Council (AIC), the U.S. private equity sector directly employed 12 million workers earning $1 trillion in wages and benefits ($80,000 per person on average) in 2022."

(https://www.privateinvestmentworks.com/2023/04/24/new-data-from-ey-and-aic-shows-private-equity-continued-to-support-workers-back-small-businesses-in-2022/)

"The U.S. private equity sector generated $1.7 trillion of U.S. gross domestic product (GDP) in 2022, comprising approximately 6.5% of total U.S. GDP.

(https://www.privateinvestmentworks.com/2023/04/24/new-data-from-ey-and-aic-shows-private-equity-continued-to-support-workers-back-small-businesses-in-2022/)

"U.S. private equity now supports 5% of America's gross domestic product (GDP), with a total economic impact of nearly $1.1 trillion. In 2018, alone, the U.S. private equity sector paid $174 billion in federal, state, and local taxes."

(https://thisisprivateequity.com/new-ey-report-shows-private-equitys-positive-impact-on-u-s-economy/)

"Over the past 20 years, private equity returns have compounded at 13.6% net of fees, compared to just 9.6% for public."

(https://www.bernstein.com/content/dam/bernstein/us/en/pdf/whitepaper/Private-Equity-the-Missing-Pillar-of-Your-Portfolio.pdf)

As you can see, PE's rise has been truly exceptional. This proliferation bodes well for business owners like you, because you have more potential buyers out there with *lots* of money to invest. Before PE existed, you had limited options to exit for millions. You basically either had to sell to a bigger competitor, give your business to your kids, or close it down. The growth of PE has directly led to a boom in entrepreneurial wealth creation.

HOW PRIVATE EQUITY WORKS

As we listen to the PE Sharks at Club Hammerhead, we discover that while PE isn't a "sport" per se, it *is* a game — and a high-stakes one at that. If you don't know the rules, you're going to lose. If you do know the rules, you'll have a good chance of winning. If you *master* the rules, you'll have a *fantastic* chance.

PE resembles a mutual fund, in that it pools money from investors for its purchases. In general, with mutual funds, the fund manager decides which stocks to buy, investors have readily available liquidity, and group investments are publicly traded. Investors can get in and out whenever they want, but they have no say in what the fund does.

A PE fund is similar but different. *For starters, it's private, not public.* And rather than only aggregate money from individual investors, it can acquire capital from pension funds, family offices, companies, even other private equity funds and firms. Also, unlike mutual funds, for mid-market firms who form the first tier of private equity, a typical minimum PE investment is as much as $5 million.

Then there's debt. As the "Great White" example showed, when a PE firm acquires a company, it uses debt to help finance the transaction. The PE firm raises capital from wealthy individuals, companies and other entities, but its acquisitions use a combination of that money plus debt. This becomes extremely important when I discuss structuring capital and similar topics in future chapters.

GPs & LPs

PE investors are called *limited partners* (LPs) because they have limited say in the PE firm's management or investments. The firm is managed by the *general partners* (GPs), and it's they who make those decisions.

LPs usually make their investments for the life of the fund *without liquidity* until such a time as it completes its mandate. PE funds are generally chartered for 5–12 years, often with an option to extend up to two years. So, when someone invests in a PE fund, that's the length of their commitment[35].

Example #2: The "Barracuda Fund"

Say an individual investor (LP) decides to invest in a PE fund[36]. Call it the "Barracuda Fund." Barracuda secures $120 million before it starts to invest. The investor commits to a $12 million investment, or 10% of the fund. Barracuda accepts that commitment but doesn't actually collect the money until the firm is ready.

Eventually, Barracuda decides to buy its first ("platform") business for $35 million. Barracuda's GPs arrived at this purchase price by taking the platform company's EBITDA of $5 million/year and multiplying that by a factor, or *industry multiple*[37], of 7. Seven times $5 million equals $35 million.

So far so good, but Barracuda might not need all that cash for the purchase. It might leverage part of it through debt. If the maximum allowable leverage to buy the platform company is 5x EBITDA, then Barracuda can finance $25 million (5x EBITDA of $5 million) of the purchase, leaving $10 million needed from its investors. Our LP investor agreed to a 10% stake in the fund, so he'll receive a *capital call*[38] for $1 million (10% of $10 million).

As Barracuda finds more companies to buy, it issues additional capital calls. Its investors are often locked in for 10–15 years, but with a goal of exiting typically within 3–7 years[39].

And we're off and running.

In summary:

- PE Fund = $120 million
- Individual investor's commitment = $12 million (10%)
- First ("platform") purchase = $35 million ($5 million EBITDA X industry multiplier of 7)
- Debt financing = $25 million (5x EBITDA)
- Cash needed from investors = $10 million
- Cash needed from individual LP = 10% of that, or $1 million.

Over time, Barracuda Fund will add relevant companies to its portfolio and issue capital calls to LPs as needed. When the LPs cash out, it's called a *distribution*[40] event. That happens only after Barracuda engages in *accelerated growth strategies* (part of the "secret playbook of private equity") to expand value. And guess what? That's the next topic at Club Hammerhead.

MULTIPLE ARBITRAGE[41]

Albert Einstein may or may not have said that *"compound interest is the most powerful force in the universe,"* but I will now argue that the most powerful force in the universe is actually something I call *multiple arbitrage*. The basic idea is this:

As the EBITDA of a business increases, so does its position within its market multiple.

In other words, as PE implements accelerated growth strategies in the businesses it acquires, not only does the EBITDA of those companies rise, the businesses hit a higher point within that industry multiplier range. Let's say the industry range is 7x-15x. As the business becomes bigger, more profitable, etc., the company in question becomes more valuable in the range, so it might demand a valuation that's perhaps 12x-15x (sometime more), which is top tier in that industry.

Using our previous example, the owner of Barracuda's platform business received a 7x industry multiple for his company's $5 million

EBITDA. If Barracuda can improve that EBITDA to $15 million after it acquires the company, then it can sell it for a 10x industry multiple. **This is a powerful concept, and it's one of the main ways that PE generates so much money for its investors.**

The question I pose to you now is this—*and this is the key part of the game!*

Why not raise your company's EBITDA now and receive the benefits of multiple arbitrage before the PE Sharks do?

If your company's current EBITDA is under $1 million, then you're looking at a multiple (on average, across most industries) between 2x and 4x. If you scale before you sell, then PE will pay a much higher multiple. Why? Because to them, scale equals more certainty and less risk. If PE Sharks are going to pay you several years of profit in a single day, then they need to feel confident that the business is going to continue to grow for the next several years. If they don't see evidence that your business is going to scale without significant effort on their part, then they're either going to pass or pay you a much lower multiple, like *a pathetic* 2x EBITDA!

This is why big *market cap*[42] companies have more stability and go public. They can operate in ways that other companies can't. In fact, they can eat up those smaller companies because they have the resources to manage change. If the markets slump, they can make redundancies, cut costs, turn off divisions, etc. Whereas a tiny business like "Bob's Windows" has no leverage. If people suddenly decide they don't want windows anymore, then Bob will either go out of business or sell his company for pennies on the dollar.

Going back to our example, let's say that within five years, Barracuda Capital (which, remember, is a *fund,* not a *firm*) has created a portfolio of companies, expanded the value of the grouping, and is ready to sell that bundle. Using advanced principles for accelerated growth and improvement, it has boosted the EBITDA on its platform business from $5 million to $15 million. That's an earnings increase of 3x over five years. The company now sells for a higher industry multiplier of 10x (versus the previous 7x), and it has an "enterprise value" of $150 million (10 x $15 million) rather than the original $35 million Barracuda paid for it.

Not only does Barracuda increase the financials of the business, it also understands that a more scaled group of companies demands a higher multiple.

To summarize:

- Original estimated value = $35 million based on 7x EBITDA of $5 million.

- New enterprise value = $150 million after implementing private equity accelerated growth strategies, based on a new EBITDA of $15 million and our new, higher industry multiplier of 10x.

This may seem like an incredible return, especially for just 5 years of investment. But I've seen it happen multiple times first-hand.

Barracuda now has its original loan of $25 million to repay, and maybe it incurred additional debt and expenses to buy bolt-on companies along the way. Let's say the loan, plus interest, legal, investment and diligence fees totals $70 million.

After Barracuda sells the company for $150 million and pays off the $70 million in debt and expenses, it's still left with $80 million to distribute. Do you know what that means? **In under five years, Barracuda's 10% limited partner would now receive an $8 million distribution on his initial $1 million investment.** That return isn't hard to calculate. It's 800%. *But remember, and this is SUPER IMPORTANT, the debt is already being paid off over the 5 or so years the company (and group) is held ... from the company profits! So, when the group eventually sells for circa $150M, the debt owned is much lower, and the investors get a bigger return, which in actuality will therefore be* ***more than $8 million****! And thus, more than an 800% return!*

But no investor simply looks at the return overall, they also look at the return based on time. And because the return each year can be different, the useful metric that averages this out so an investor can make decisions is called the *compound annual growth rate* or CAGR.

> "The compound annual growth rate (CAGR) is the mean annual growth rate of an investment over a period longer than one year. It's one of the most accurate ways to calculate and determine returns for individual assets, investment portfolios, and anything that can rise or fall in value over time."[43]

The formula for calculating our CAGR is as follows:

$$\text{CAGR} = ((\text{EV}/\text{BV})^{1/n} - 1) \times 100$$

... where *EV* is the end value, *BV* the beginning value, and *n* the number of years.

We divide our end value of $8M by our beginning value of $1M and get $8M. We then calculate $8M by an exponent of 1/5 or 0.2 to get 1.5157, then subtract 1 to get 0.5157, and multiply by 100 to express the CAGR as a %, leaving us with a 51.57% compound annual growth rate (!).

$$CAGR = ((EV/BV)^{1/n} - 1) \times 100$$

$$CAGR = ((\$8M/\$1M)^{1/5} - 1) \times 100$$

$$CAGR = (\$8M^{0.2} - 1) \times 100$$

$$CAGR = (1.5157 - 1) \times 100$$

$$CAGR = 0.5157 \times 100$$

$$CAGR = 51.57\%$$

Fabulous! In fact, I typically work with small-cap to mid-cap companies (companies with total market value or total market capitalization runs from about $250 million to $2 billion (small-cap) or all the way from $2 billion to $10 billion (mid-cap)). And *Investopedia* agrees this is a great CAGR:

> "What Is a Good CAGR? For companies with large capitalization, a CAGR in sales of 5% to 12% is good. For small-cap and midcap companies, a CAGR of 15% to 30% is good. Startup companies, on the other hand, should have a CAGR ranging from 100% to 500%."[44]

How did Barracuda create this wealth? It did the following:

- Aggregated several relevant companies and assets.
- Improved structures, practices, leadership and talent across the board.
- Boosted EBITDA from $5 million to $15 million.
- Boosted the multiple from 7x to 10x by creating a more scalable business.
- Sold the company for $150 million.
- Paid financing and fees of $70 million ... and again, the $70M comes from company profits and not from the investors' coffers! So, their actual return is higher. *Welcome to the mad world of private equity!*

Our hypothetical individual investor does have to pay a few fees. A 2% annual management fee to the PE firm to cover its operating costs is common. Once an investor's contracted *minimum rate of return* or *preferred return*[45] is realized, it's also common to pay 20% of all profits (called *carried interest*[46]) back to the PE firm. This is how the firms and their partners create their own wealth[47]. To give their personnel a vested interest in their outcomes, PE firms will also generally allow employees to invest in their own funds.

TYPES OF PE FIRMS

PE firms have grown not only in number, but also in type. They can have thousands of employees and funds in the tens of billions, such as Blackstone and Carlyle. Or they can be small, with only a few employees and a relatively modest fund size under $100 million. As you might imagine, the number of individuals with the millions needed to become private equity LPs is limited. So, all PE firms compete assertively for investors.

Smaller firms usually run only one or two funds at a time so they can focus on current priorities. Larger, global firms with armies of investors and specialists usually manage multiple funds and tap into a variety of industries and verticals. Some firms stipulate that they must purchase all *anchor holdings* or *platform companies* within the first seven years or so, while others have no such limitation.

Generally, PE firms issue quarterly financial reports that disclose what and where money has been invested, which funds have been returned or distributed, and current values. At Annual General Meetings, general partners (and perhaps CEOs and other leaders) will present to limited partners and answer their questions. I've been involved in many of these, and I've made my share of presentations to investors as a CEO.

Types of PE Funds

Some exclusive PE funds, such as *family offices* or *pension funds,* require no outside investors. These funds have far fewer stipulations and time requirements compared to the examples we've discussed.

More common fund types include:

- ***Buyout funds.*** These funds buy a controlling stake in more seasoned and established businesses. They usually perform more reliably than other funds, with more conservative results. Buyout funds replace the previous majority stakeholder and become "the boss," or controlling partner.

- ***Growth equity funds.*** These funds invest in mature companies going through transformations with high growth potential. Many private equity firms now offer *growth equity*, where a fund will put a small amount of money into a business it potentially wants to acquire in the future. It's like a venture fund, except the companies are generally more mature, so the business is more profitable than a typical venture fund.

- ***Venture capital funds.*** These funds usually buy a small stake in a newer business (often tech-related) that presents a "high risk/high reward" scenario. They're usually more speculative *and* more creative, and the company's existing CEO likely remains in place.

- *Pooled co-investing.* A PE fund will sometimes do this if it finds a larger-than-usual investment target. In it, several funds band together. One takes a controlling interest. And they usually share in the decision-making.

- *Limited partner co-investing.* Similar to the above, this is where a fund might pull off a larger-than-usual investment by inviting one or more limited partners to make separate, additional investments in a business.

- *Private debt funds.* To avoid conflicts of interest, this is where larger PE firms might lend to other portfolio companies backed by private equity. These funds count as leverage in buying platforms and acquisitions, or they fund operations.

- *A fund of funds.* These are used when investors want to be more diversified. Think of them as a mutual fund that invests in different private equity funds.

EVALUATING FIRMS & FUNDS

A PE firm is categorized by the first year it makes an investment, which is called its *vintage*. This helps investors make "apples to apples" (or "grapes to grapes") comparisons among firms because it factors in economic and other external factors that may affect performance. Independent firms then place PE firms into one of four *quartiles*: upper, upper-middle, lower-middle and lower.

PE firms are also ranked according to three key metrics:

1. **Internal Rate of Return (IRR):** This is the most important metric in private equity. It ranks the net return earned by a PE firm's investors over a certain time period expressed as a percentage (%). IRR is mainly about speed of return vs. the overall return amount. IRR factors in capital calls, fees for carried interest, and distributions. With it, you can compare a PE investment with, say, investments in stocks and real estate. Net of all charges and fees, PE firms typically yield annual returns around roughly 15%, outperforming stocks and real estate.

2. **Multiple on Invested Capital (MOIC):** Mentioned earlier, this metric represents cash return. One main difference between IRR and MOIC is that MOIC does *not* take into account time or an investor's holding period. In our example above, where a $1 million investment enjoyed an $8 million return, that would translate to an MOIC of 8x, or "8x MOIC." Unlike IRR, this figure doesn't take into account whether the return took 12 months or 12 years to obtain. It's the overall return, not how long it takes to achieve the return.

3. **Distributions to Paid-in Capital (DPI):** This is the ratio of money paid in to a fund against the amount distributed. DPI starts at zero and breaks even sooner or later at "1" as distributions are made. As a fund becomes more active, the DPI shows how quickly it's returning money to investors.

All three of these metrics are important in evaluating funds. In fact, with over 5,000 funds to choose from, they're more important than ever. You should know how common PE fund types relate to your own investment style, and which will best serve you and your business.

Back to Club Hammerhead ...

Which of these metrics are the PE Sharks talking mostly about? MOIC. They love to brag about this number. If you came in one night and announced you'd helped one of your groups or portfolio companies exit at 2x or 3x MOIC, the PE Sharks would laugh you out of the club. But if you sold for 5x, 6x or even 7x MOIC, you wouldn't have to pay for a drink the entire night.

IRR is important. But to a PE Shark, MOIC is where the game is played. It's the number on the scoreboard, and it's what their bonuses are mainly tied to.

WHY IS PRIVATE EQUITY IMPORTANT?

We've established that private equity is unique in its ability to create the kind of accelerated growth and transferability that leads to a high-value exit. Whether you're an owner, entrepreneur, CEO or executive, PE is likely to appear on your radar.

In the bigger picture, however, multiple entities sit in what we describe as the *capital markets*[48], and private money goes into growing and scaling companies in different stages of investments. Pictured as a scale, it looks something like this:

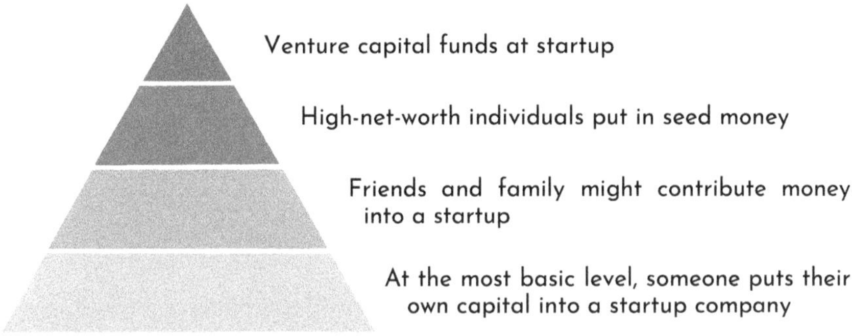

This is about the early stages of a business, possibly transitioning into its scale-up phase, and these situations involve *spread betting*: People put small amounts of money into different entities, betting that at least one will eventually succeed and create a large capital event. It's like putting chips on a roulette table. The big payday is placing them all on "black 35." Here, you're spreading them around to create a lower reward but with lower risk.

In the venture capital world, 3 or 4 out of 10 bets might work to some degree. Some will return what investors put in; the rest might not work out at all. But when you move up the chain into private equity, those bigger PE firms and funds have certain protocols they have to adhere to. More often than not, they're investing in solid companies that are through the startup phase. These companies are valuable because they're profitable. Fewer investments, but each has a higher likelihood of return.

Say a PE firm has a $300–$400 million fund. Whereas a VC might invest in hundreds of businesses, a PE firm will only invest in 8–12. But the PE firms are more embedded in those businesses. They'll install a board of directors. They'll have operating partners. They'll provide services to boost the company's value. Will they still experience a few misses here and there? Yes. But they'll expect 7 out of 10 (or more) of their investments to work.

Unlike VCs, PE firms will also raise value by bolting on other companies *vertically* or *horizontally*:

- Expanding a business ***horizontally*** means buying competitors. Someone owns a car manufacturing business, and they buy another car brand.
- Expanding ***vertically*** (or *vertical integration*) is going up and down the supply or value chains. It's not buying another car brand. It's buying a dealer or a servicing division, adding elements both up and down that create a group doing multiple things across multiple geographies within a broader industry.

PE executes horizontal and vertical expansion like no other entity, and this strategy alone has the power to increase business values exponentially.

Private Equity Mindset

Most business owners are emotionally attached to what they've created. Your business is your baby. The PE Sharks around your table in Club Hammerhead don't have that attachment. Your business is an asset they may or may not leverage. In fact, they're going to use your emotional attachment to your business *against you.*

The PE Shark mindset is militaristic. They have a job to do, and casualties are inevitable. Nothing is more important than *the mission,* and they want *predictable, repeatable, and sustainable performance* vs. randomness or uncertainty. Everything must be intentional. Calculated. Precise. They go on these missions again and again with a high rate of success. That's why they're millionaires and billionaires.

Just because you're good at growing a business doesn't mean you'll be good at selling it. To win, you need to match the PE Sharks' clinical, methodical and militaristic mindset. You must shift your thinking. You might want to hire a specialist advisor or coach who understands the PE world. And you'll need to adopt a frame of mind for *bridging deltas in value and profit.* By *deltas,* I mean the difference between your current and desired business value, and your current and desired profit. Let's talk about that.

BRIDGING DELTAS

When I pitch my exit planning services to business owners, I ask them one question:

> "Which would you rather do: Spend the rest of your life working in your business, chasing one customer after the other, living with the reality that things could change in an instant putting your livelihood at risk ... or put in the work now to create a high-value business that you could sell for a life-changing amount of money 3–5 years from now, and spend the rest of your life reaping the rewards of your hard work?"

Since you're reading this book, it's safe to assume you'd rather do the latter. You want to exit your business while you still have the time and energy to live your best life. This task doesn't end at creating an income-producing business, or even a sellable one. You have to make sure that the sale actually happens on favourable terms to you.

I help my clients do this by identifying the existing deltas in their business and optimizing them. I know what sophisticated buyers are looking for, and I have a wealth of experience getting granular with the growth and value expansion plans of hundreds of different clients. And I've helped all of them achieve the outcome they wanted.

First, you'll need to get clear on what I call the *profit bridge*. This is the profitability difference between your company and comparable companies in your industry. Looking at your profit bridge helps you find ways to improve your financial performance and overall efficiency.

Say your business currently nets $2 million in EBITDA and $10 million in total revenue. Your profit margin is 20%. Now look at businesses in the same market or in your current geography. You might find a company doing $10 million in top line revenue but $3 million in profit, so a 30% profit margin. They're probably operating more efficiently than you are, which means you have an opportunity to bridge that delta and become the most profitable business in your industry, or at the very lowest, comparable.

Next, you'll need to address the *value bridge*. While the profit bridge speaks to your company's financial performance, the value bridge *determines your multiple*. That, more than anything, determines what the PE Sharks are willing to pay for your business.

Say your numbers look pretty good right now. As in our earlier example, you're making $2 million in profit. To figure out what you can sell your business for, you need to take a hard look at how well it's built and operated beyond your financial statements.

You *won't* be able to command a high multiple from private equity if:

- Your internal processes aren't documented.
- Your business is overly reliant on your personal relationship with certain customers.
- You only have a few customers driving the majority of your revenue.

If any of these factors ring true, the PE Sharks will say, "Your business is okay but high risk, it might not generate the same value after an ownership change. We'd better play it safe and offer the lowest possible multiple." If your industry's prevailing low-end multiple is 4x EBITDA, then the Sharks will offer you $8 million for your business.

On the other hand, you *will* be able to command a high multiple as long as:

- All your company's internal workings are documented.
- You could step back for weeks, and the business would run just as smoothly as if you were around.
- Your business makes good money without being overly reliant on certain customers.

In this case, the PE Sharks will say, "This business runs like a well-oiled machine, so it'll do just as well after the ownership change." They'll happily offer you the high end of your industry's prevailing multiple, say 8x EBITDA, for a sale price of $16 million.

Which sounds better to you: $8 million or $16 million?

You can't control the prevailing multiples in your industry, but you can control where your business falls within the range by looking back in Part One, at the "15 Characteristics of a High-Value Business" section again and start to improve the value delta in your business by improving those areas. This will give the best chance of hitting the highest multiple within your industry's range.

THE FIVE LEVERS[49] OF VALUE EXPANSION

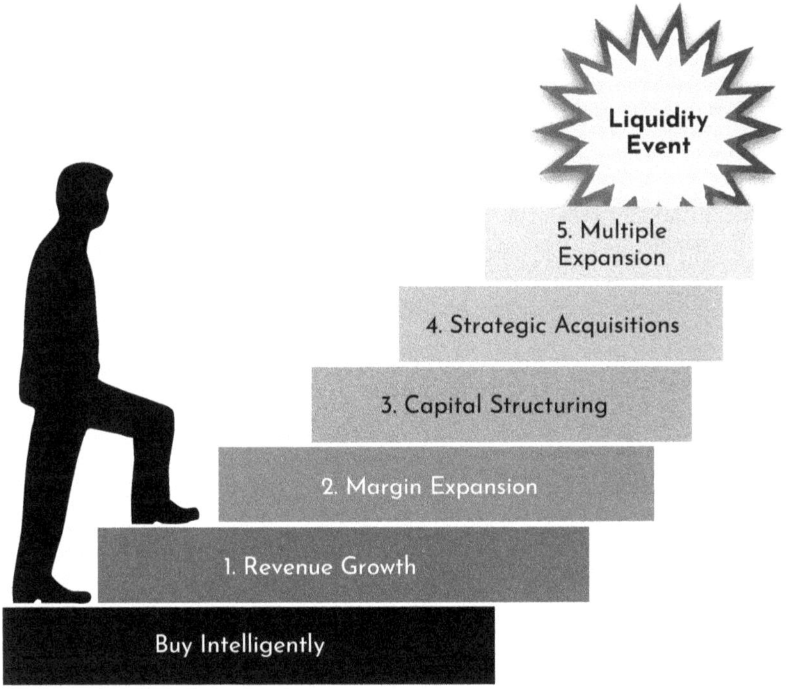

The graphic above is the most important one in this book. It represents *value expansion*: how private equity buys a business, scales it, exits it, and creates a hell of a lot of money in a short timeframe.

You might look at some of these steps and think, "I know that. We do that." But trust me: PE does it with a focus and precision you won't find anywhere else.

As we previously discussed, PE Sharks judge themselves on MOIC (multiple on invested capital). As a refresher:

- Say a PE firm buys a business for $30 million and puts another $30 million into it. Their total investment is $60 million.
- They now expect to make a 3–5x return (MOIC) on that investment. That's $180 million–$300 million.
- They expect to accomplish this in 3–7 years ideally, though they'll wait up to 10 years (or the life of the fund) to make their investors happy and make more money for them if a particular investment is performing beyond expectation.

Most entrepreneurs and business owners think the best way to maximize ROI is to scale their business intentionally but slowly, not taking big risks. They then get stuck on the "scale up" treadmill for years. They assume PE must practice some kind of alchemy or dark art to achieve its high performance. But there's nothing magical about how PE scales businesses. The difference is the sheer amount of effort and strategy the Sharks put into value expansion. The whole end-to-end strategy is called the "buy and build."

After PE buys a business "intelligently" — for the cheapest possible price to maximize MOIC — it uses five levers to expand value. The first two represent "organic growth." They create revenue and profit that's typically re-invested, or in the case of PE ownership, used to pay back debt. There's nothing wrong with these strategies, but they can be long and gruelling.

That's why PE goes beyond them to the next three levers, which create "strategic growth."

Let's get into it.

LEVER #1: REVENUE GROWTH

This lever is about growing revenues by building a sound marketing strategy to bolster sales. You're probably already doing this in your business to some extent. If not, it might be more of a profitable hobby or passion project. In any case, it pays to revisit your revenue growth strategies to make sure you're on track with your revenue targets.

To bolster your revenue, you can:

1. Bring in new customers.
2. Increase your prices.
3. Have your existing customers buy *more* from you (cross-sell, up-sell).
4. Have your existing customers buy *more frequently* from you (repeat sales).
5. Develop new products and/or services.
6. Expand your *total addressable market* (TAM[50], the biggest part of the universe you can go after).
7. Find more champagne customers[51].

I'll leave it to you to figure out which of these strategies can best grow your revenue, but here's a pro tip: Combine a few of these strategies together to maximize your results.

LEVER #2: MARGIN EXPANSION

Growing revenue is meaningless if your costs grow at the same rate. That's where *margin expansion* comes in. If you want to build a business that runs without you, you have to continually create more revenue while also driving efficiency and optimizing costs.

To expand your margins, you can:

1. Raise prices.

2. Cut direct and variable costs (e.g. staff, supplier agreements, overheads, streamlining operations via technology and automation).

How efficiently is your business running? Are you paying for things you don't need? Do certain processes take your team too long to complete and slow the inflow of profits? If so, you might want to explore using technology and automation to fix these issues and increase your profit margins.

Once your revenue growth is as strong as it can be, and your spending is as controlled as it can be, you can do what PE does best: couple *organic growth* with *strategic growth* to achieve *exponential growth.*

Strategic growth is where you start to leverage capital. As we'll cover in Part Three (Scale To Sale™ Methodology), that could be leveraging debt or acquiring equity in a business — be it bringing in investors or scaling through joint ventures and acquisitions.

These next three levers represent the strategic growth tactics that PE does better than anyone else.

> "Exponential growth is the compounding effect when combining organic and strategic growth strategies, the result being an increase in both scale and speed of growth. By combining organic and strategic growth strategies, you get there faster, and you get a bigger result."

Lever #3: Capital Structuring

Private equity firms do something that many entrepreneurs shy away from: leverage debt. They embrace debt because they know there's a cost to growth: "You need money to make money."

When money is cheap, like when interest rates are low, PE owners take on a significant amount of debt. They do this strategically so they can make acquisitions at low prices, thus making it easier to compound their investments fast.

Most business owners are taught to avoid debt at all costs, but this mentality has historically slowed the growth of countless companies. If you want to achieve a high-value exit by selling to private equity, start thinking like a PE Shark.

The sharks at Club Hammerhead care about MOIC. That means having top access to capital as efficiently as possible. If you borrow a heap of money at low interest rates and acquire businesses cheaply, then expand their value using the techniques in this book, you'll have a much better chance of boosting your own MOIC and attracting PE money.

Should you go crazy and take on every loan you're qualified for, regardless of the conditions? No. Sometimes you should avoid debt, like when interest rates are high. But many businesses are *under-capitalized* and can't take advantage of growth opportunities. If you find capital available at a relatively low interest rate, then consider accessing it to buy more resources quickly, scale more quickly and give yourself a huge strategic advantage over entrepreneurs who don't understand the debt-leverage game.

Keep in mind: PE firms are experts at leveraging debt, but they're also very good at *paying it down*. The latter increases value even more by reducing liabilities. So be smart in taking on debt but be even smarter in paying it down. To truly *leverage debt*, you have to do both.

LEVER #4: STRATEGIC ACQUISITIONS

No private equity firm buys a business and then sits on it. The PE Sharks at Club Hammerhead buy companies so they can bolt them together into rollups that maximize their combined value.

Welcome to the world of *strategic acquisitions.*

Acquisitions are the fastest way to scale, period. They're also a fantastic way to expand value. You can literally double or triple a business overnight as you build an entity around what you currently have.

Say you've achieved good organic growth and optimized your business through technology and automation. Now it's time to drive up your value even more by buying other companies. PE calls these "bolt-on acquisitions" because they bolt businesses onto their original acquisition (platform). The goal is to add either competitors or businesses up and down the supply chain (*horizontal or vertical integration*) to grow value exponentially. In your world, you might buy a supplier, or the means of production. Or maybe you'll buy your biggest rival. The point is to form a group of businesses that create a larger and more valuable entity.

Why is a group entity so much more valuable? Because businesses that have greater scale also generally carry lower *risk*. They have more assets that can be managed in challenging times, and more assets that can be managed in *good* times. Put simply, scale matters. Anything small is risky. And Club Hammerhead doesn't like risk, especially risk it can't manage and control.

Look at your own business. Say you already have a strong customer base. What other products or services might they need or want? If those assets exist in another company, you could acquire it and add those products to your platform. You might also buy a company to acquire their people. Apple has bought hundreds of businesses over the last 10 years, many so they could acquire their *talent*—people who can further accelerate Apple's growth strategies.

Acquiring another company can jack up your value far faster than developing a whole new product line. Yes, it takes time to integrate another business into yours, but it's often the most efficient way to boost value. Coca Cola grows its product line largely by buying other beverage companies. Why? Because it's more efficient to buy Vitamin Water than to create that product internally, and it's also much lower risk to have someone test the market for you before jumping in yourself.

LEVER #5: MULTIPLE EXPANSION

This lever is the most important one in PE's secret playbook. When PE buys a company, as we have discussed, it usually does so for a *multiple* of that company's profit. Who decides that multiple? Generally speaking, it falls within the range of multiples in the current capital markets.

Where your business falls in that range is entirely in your control.

I touched on this in Part One, and I'll take you through the nitty-gritty of getting a high multiple in Part Three. But for now, I just want you to understand the basic factors that determine a profit multiple so you can reverse engineer your business to achieve the highest one.

When I do exit strategy planning for a company, we look at profitability, but we really focus on *multiple expansion.* Because when that happens, you can experience a huge payday. And remember:

A successful exit *will be* the largest financial event of your life.

Start Expanding the Value of Your Business *Now*

Why am I so passionate about helping business owners achieve the high-value exit of their dreams? Because I've seen it happen, and it's life changing.

The inside information I'm giving you in this book isn't just theory; it's reality. Take this example:

PE Purchase of "Company X"[52]

- Twelve (12) acquisitions bolted together
- Over $2 billion exit valuation
- 14x profit multiple

This describes an actual acquisition I was involved in as the CEO of a private equity–backed company's international division. We sold this business, this *group*, to one of the world's largest PE firms at a price of over *14 years of profit in a single day*.

Imagine if that was your business. Imagine the liquidity event you'd experience. Imagine how much your life would change.

If you want to get there, you have to think and act like the private equity firms. And while PE employs a mix of everything we've discussed in this chapter, its success is also about *how* it pulls together those five value expansion levers. PE is clinical, precise and disciplined — so much so that my time in that world felt like serving in a military special operations unit.

PE is built to perform at a high level in a compressed timeframe, and I'm 100% confident that if you use their levers to achieve value expansion *before* they swoop in, you'll achieve a huge advantage over your competitors.

You already own your own business, so in PE terms, you already have your "platform." You probably also have organic growth nailed in those first two levers, because all businesses try to grow their revenue while controlling their costs[53]. If that's the case, then it's time to explore *strategic growth* — to pull those last three levers that have transformed thousands of private equity investors into millionaires and billionaires.

As we prepare to leave Club Hammerhead, take a final look around. Those cigar-puffing PE Sharks have no idea what they're in for when they try to buy your business. Why?

Because you're one section in this book away from knowing as much as they do.

You're a few dozen pages from being able to look a PE Shark in the eye and know that you're the prize and not the prey.

And you're a few minutes away from being equipped to experience a liquidity event that will change your life.

KEY TAKEAWAYS

- Private equity is where private individuals or institutions invest money in a firm for the purpose of acquiring businesses, bolting them together, and selling them for significantly more money than they initially invested.
- PE firms can be large (with fund sizes in the tens of billions) or small (with a fund size under $100 million).
- PE firms are categorized by vintage, or the first year a fund makes an investment.
- The number of PE funds has exploded from 24 in 1980 to nearly 20,000 in 2022. From 2000–2022, PE firms' assets under management (AUM) has grown from $579 billion to about $7.8 trillion.
- PE investors are called limited partners (LPs). The firm is the general partner (GP).
- As you increase a company's EBITDA, you also increase its multiple within its market range. This is called multiple arbitrage.
- Types of PE firms include buyout funds, growth equity funds, venture capital funds, pooled co-investing, limited partner co-investing, private debt funds and funds of funds.
- Buyout funds are the most popular PE funds. These funds buy a controlling stake in more established businesses and usually perform more reliably than other funds.
- You can evaluate a PE fund's effectiveness by looking at its Internal Rate of Return (IRR), Multiple on Invested Capital (MOIC) and Distributions to Paid-in Capital (DPI). PE Sharks care most about MOIC.
- PE firms can raise value by bolting on other companies vertically or horizontally. Horizontally means buying

competitors. Vertically means buying companies up and down the supply or value chain.

- PE investors commonly pay a 2% annual management fee on their investment to the PE firm to cover its operating costs.
- Once a PE investor's contracted minimum rate of return or preferred return is realized, they will commonly pay 20% of all profits (called carried interest) back to the PE firm. This is how the firms and their partners create their wealth.
- Your profit bridge is the difference between your profitability and that of comparable businesses in your industry.
- Your value bridge determines the multiple that a PE firm will pay for your business.
- Private equity uses five levers of value expansion: Revenue Growth, Margin Expansion, Capital Structuring, Strategic Acquisitions, Multiple Expansion.
- The first two levers represent "organic growth." The last three involve "strategic growth."

PART THREE

SCALE TO SALE™ METHODOLOGY

OVERVIEW

SCALE TO SALE™ is the proprietary methodology I developed to scale companies (and their owners) to the high-value exits they deserve. Based on what I learned from a decade in private equity, it consists of five steps designed to empower entrepreneurs and business owners to feel 100% confident as they sit across the table from the Private Equity Sharks.

Here's what it looks like…

Scale To Sale™ Methodology

1. Establish a Clear End Game.

We begin with the end in mind, then reverse engineer.

2. Strengthen Foundations.

We ensure that your core business fundamentals are in place.

3. Scale Fast & Expand Value.

We apply the potent combination of capital structuring, high-value partnerships, and scale via mergers and acquisitions (M&A).

4. Profit Up.

We prepare and position your business before going to market.

5. Exit for the Highest Multiple.

We go through the end-to-end sales process, with an emphasis on sell-side control and winning the game.

STEP 1: ESTABLISH A CLEAR END GAME

"A goal is something you come from, not something you work towards."

I love the above quote, because it gets to the heart of reverse engineering your business. Instead of seeing your end game as the destination, view it as your starting point. Clarity in goals breeds clarity in methods. Once you've identified the end game, you can outline the path back to your current reality and see the steps you'll need to take to reach your ideal exit.

To win the PE game and achieve what you want personally and financially, you need to start from the *end goal* and work your way backwards. Once your end game is clear, then the other Scale To Sale™ Methodology steps will be more effective.

PE Sharks never start an initiative without a clear end game in mind: the value they want to realize for their shareholders after they buy, scale and exit a business. For example, if a PE firm buys a company and wants to sell it for 10x or 12x its current profit, they might buy other businesses and merge them together. The exact timeframe of the sale depends on their access to capital, the dynamics of the business, and its potential for growth by delaying selling, but it's typically 3–7 years.

By the end of this step, my wish for you is this:

- You're clear on your "**life-changing number**" and your desired net worth when you exit.
- You understand your wealth **delta**—the difference between your current wealth and where you want it to be upon exiting.
- You have a **vision** for your business that will survive even if you leave, and you accept the fact that you may not be there to see that vision through.
- You know your **options** in terms of how you exit, whether you're leaving the business, so you have more time and freedom, staying in the company in some form, or a combination of both.

THE "LIFE-CHANGING NUMBER"

When I work with business owners and entrepreneurs who are planning to sell and exit their companies, I ask them three powerful questions. Their answers form the guideposts that will keep them on track throughout the Scale to Sale™ process:

1. *What is your life-changing number?*
2. *Why does it matter?*
3. *Where are you now?*

"WHAT'S MY LIFE-CHANGING NUMBER?"

Your *life-changing number* is your financial freedom figure. It's the amount of money it'll take to make life comfortable, secure and fulfilling for you and your heirs. It will free you to afford all material needs and wants, fulfil deep-seated purposes and perhaps create generational wealth. This number varies from person to person, and I never judge the figure a client chooses.

Be sure that, once invested, your life-changing number will yield abundant income on a monthly basis (after likely deductions) and that your wealth will continue to grow.

As you consider your life-changing number, you might discover a *wealth delta*: the difference between your current net worth and what you need it to be once you exit your business. Say your current net worth is $3 million and your life-changing number is $20 million net, after tax. That means your wealth delta is $17 million.

This number is useful to you, if not to private equity, because it defines the target outcome or multiple from selling your business. If your *wealth bridge* is $17 million, then your high-value exit will need to be at least that number after taxes and other payments related to the sale. This is not the enterprise value of your business, so assuming you pay capital gains tax at 25%, you need to sell your business for at least $25-$30 million to bridge your wealth delta.

"Why Does That Number Really Matter?"

Entrepreneurs have different goals for going into business. It might be material comfort, a more purposeful life, travel, making the world a better place, or establishing and growing generational wealth. The one word that comes up time and again with business owners is *freedom.* However, you define that word, chances are your life-changing number will help get you there.

Your "why" is about your true values and purpose in life. I like supporting children in third-world countries who don't have access to western society's resources, especially education. But my true *why* is my family — my wife Carrie and my two daughters, Arabella and Matilda. I want to make sure they have an amazing life, that I can support them to the best of my ability, and that I can be a role model for my daughters.

It's also good to have a *big, hairy, audacious goal* (BHAG). When I transitioned from "buy and breakup" private equity into a more entrepreneurial and positive mission 7 years ago, I asked myself, *If you could do just one extraordinary thing, what would it be?* I smiled as I wrote on my vision board: "Buy the Boston Celtics." I started playing basketball when I was six, and I've always loved Celtics legend Larry Bird. I watched the Celtics dominate the NBA in the '80s and '90s, and I enjoyed watching them win again in 2024.

Just for fun, I went as far as looking into what the Celtics last sold for, which was somewhere around $300 million. (Today, the price tag would likely be more like $3 *billion*.) And then I went a step further. I called someone connected with the actual owner of an NBA basketball team, and I had an illuminating conversation with that person about what it takes to buy a team. I'm not a billionaire yet, but I do have a 20-year vision to buy the Boston Celtics. To get to that *big, hairy, audacious goal,* how much change would I have to make in the world? How many lives would I have to impact? And who would I need to become?

Truth be told, I don't care that much about owning the Boston Celtics. I care about what it would feel like to write the check to buy them. To get to that point, I'd have to make a heap of positive change in the world and become *who I need to be*. That's what it's really about: *How would you have to grow as a person to reach your most ambitious goal?*

Your own *why* might be philanthropic. It might be about having experiences. It might be purely material. No judgement!

"Is What I'm Doing Now Going to Get Me to My Life-Changing Number?"

Most millionaires and billionaires got that way because they did the work. Their businesses became great because they became great, too.

If the answer to the above question is no, then you have to change your number or change what you're doing to reach it. Start by asking yourself how you might alter what you're doing on a daily basis to get on the right path. How can you accelerate things to get faster results?

This isn't necessarily about "getting rich quick." That's certainly a goal in the PE world, but "getting rich easy" isn't — no matter what you see on social media from so-called "gurus." Rather than focusing on shortcutting time, focus on your education, your network, delivering quantifiable value, creating leverage and getting in the "reps."

Pace is important, but it doesn't happen by magic. PE pros can *compress time* because they do the work.

CREATE YOUR VIVID VISION[54]

When I work with clients on the Clear End Game exercise, we determine what their business is worth today, as well as the *exit vision* we're building towards. The Vivid Vision exercise is about how the business needs to look and feel so the owner feels ready and happy to sell.

A Vivid Vision is far more precise than a traditional vision or mission statement, and it's more than just a number. It's not just about getting your business to a value of, say, $30 million. It's about envisioning what the company is *like* at that point. What's the culture? What sort of people are on board? What kinds of customers are you working with?

The more detail and colour you can add to your vision, the more compelling it'll be, and the more you can use it to attract the talent that will accomplish it. "CEO Whisperer" Cameron Herold has a goal to make Vivid Visions common in businesses everywhere. In one of his examples, he talks about building a house. You have an architect, contractors, and a whole host of people involved. The architect doesn't come up with something random; they base their designs on what you want. Three bedrooms? A pool? A garage? Floor-to-ceiling windows?

I highly recommend Cameron Herold's excellent book, *Vivid Vision.* For our purposes, we want more than just a "picture," as so many vision boards seem to be based upon. A picture says a thousand words, but your thousand words — your interpretation — could be much different than mine. A Vivid Vision forces you to write in detail every aspect of what that business needs to look like in the future. How much revenue is your business generating? How profitable is it? What geography does it work across? How many people are employed there? What's the culture, the marketing strategy? How do we build products and solutions?

You'll end up with a four-to-six-page document that you can always refer back to when you discover your voids, deltas and needed resources. In the words of Cameron Herold:

> "Creating a Vivid Vision brings the future into the present, so we can have clarity on what we are building now. It is a detailed overview of what my business will look like, feel like and act like three years out — by December 31st, 202X. Sharing it with others helps it become reality! Because of their clarity, CEOs globally are using Vivid Visions instead of the traditional Mission or Vision Statements, and COOs are helping to ensure they become reality."
>
> —Cameron Herold[55]

Here's how a Vivid Vision looks compared to a standard corporate vision:

Regular Vision

"I want to own the most popular independent real estate brokerage in Sacramento."

Vivid Vision

"In three years, I want everyone to recognize our distinctive blue 'for sale' signs. I'll exit the business for $50 million, and it'll continue to be seen as the most innovative brokerage in its space."

Your Vivid Vision should paint a picture of your company's future after you're no longer a part of it. In fact, one of the first things you'll be asked when you decide you want to sell your company is, "Tell me your vision of the business." Your Vivid Vision is for you, but it's also a roadmap to what you're building toward and what a prospective buyer is going to continue building once they take ownership.

I'm often asked, "If I want to sell my business in the next 12 to 36 months, then why am I creating a vision for it in the future?" Answers:

- It will help you make the right decisions over the next few years to make your business even more valuable.
- You can easily share the vision.
- You can use it to *de-risk* the business.
- It gives you a map of what you're building towards.

- One of the most important things you have to do when selling your business (covered in "Step 4: Profit Up") is create your Exit Story, and that comes directly from your Vivid Vision.

EVALUATE YOUR EXIT OPTIONS

You have two basic options in exiting your business:

1. Transition your leadership role.
2. Sell.

Transitioning your leadership role basically means exiting your business without selling it. For example, you can remove yourself as the CEO, hire and groove in a new one, then join the board.

If you do choose to *sell*, then you have many more considerations. Of course, you can sell to private equity. But you can also sell to another corporation, publicly list your company, or even sell to your current employees.

The best way to look at your selling options is to divide them into *internal* and *external sales.*

With **internal sales**:

- You can sell the company to your ***partner***.

- You can sell it to your ***management*** team.
- Similar to these first two options, you can do a ***management buyout*** (MBO) or ***management buy-in*** (MBI). An MBO is when the management team comes together and buys out the exiting shareholders. An MBI is when some of the management team and usually an external third party come together to buy out existing shareholders.
- You can sell it back to your ***employees***.

These options tend to be quite favourable to smaller businesses that aren't as attractive to the bigger capital market investors.

With **external sales**, your business has a certain amount of size and scale to it. In this case, you can sell it to a *strategic buyer*[56] or *financial buyer*[57]. That means selling to another company, likely a private equity firm. You might also sell to a private company that's *backed* by a PE firm, or a *PE-backed strategic*[58].

Just to fully clarify here:

- A *strategic buyer* is another company or corporation.
- A *financial buyer* is an entity like a PE firm or family office.

A *PE-backed strategic* is a company already owned by a PE firm ... so in essence it's a company buying another company, but the money is coming via the PE capital markets.

I'm sometimes asked about other external exits, such as listing a company on a stock exchange or going public (as with an IPO). Those aren't really exits, they're predominantly a capital raise. They're also incredibly complex, can be highly expensive, and don't always deliver the best outcome. For example, you usually can't liquidate your involvement straight away. You're locked in.

In short, if you want to achieve a high-value exit that's going to change your life, your best bet is either a *financial exit* or a *strategic exit.*

If you want to sell your business outright for the maximum amount of money and get gobbled up by another company, then you should probably target a strategic exit because they tend to pay the most. However, a financial exit with a buyer like a PE firm offers an important perk: the option to buy back into the firm.

For example:

- PE firm buys your company for $30M.
- It then allows you to roll over 15% into the new entity that's created post sale ($4.5M).
- That company sells for $120M in 5 years' time.
- Simple math = your investment is now worth $18M

You've effectively sold your company twice!

If you want to keep going down that route, you can partner with one of *those* acquirers, invest your rollover equity in those businesses, and keep growing your company. Who knows? It could become the next Apple or Amazon.

STEP 2: STRENGTHEN YOUR FOUNDATIONS

I'll cover scaling and expanding value in Steps 3 and 4, but this step is about the fundamentals. You need to know the value of your business today, then determine what it could be worth in the future so you can bridge that delta. Fixing issues and strengthening foundations is called *de-risking.*

Assessing Your Business Now & in the Future

A. What is your business worth today?

Before we put a value on your business, you need to understand *business valuations.* That starts with learning the difference between *financial value* and *strategic value,* then talking about *multiples.*

Financial Value vs. Strategic Value

Valuations used to be purely financial instruments based on accounting principles dating back to the 1950s and 1960s. Today, they've evolved. I won't go through the complexities of different valuation analyses here (I discuss them in many of my podcast episodes), but what you really need to know is the difference between *financial value* and *strategic value.*

Financial value is about the expectations given your current plans and strategies, expressed as EBITDA times your multiple. Why EBITDA rather than a *revenue* multiple? Private equity is interested in cash flowing businesses, and cash is a by-product of profitability whereas revenue is really a demonstration of growth, with or without profit.

Strategic value refers to the value of your business once new strategies and intangible assets are developed in your business — notably those found in this book — are implemented.

It might sound obvious — financial value sets the baseline, but strategic value drives the multiple. Both combined create your valuation.

(Enterprise) Multiples

Let's take a deeper dive into multiples.

> Enterprise multiple ... is a ratio used to determine the value of a company ... Enterprise multiples can vary depending on the industry. Higher enterprise multiples are expected in high-growth industries and lower multiples in industries with slow growth.[59]

A multiple is literally a multiplier of your current performance and your expected performance in the future. As referenced earlier, PE will use EBITDA as the key metric for this, which is the single biggest driver of value when you sell your business. Different industries have different ranges of multiples. And as we've discussed in *multiple arbitrage,* your particular multiple will vary based on the size, scale and other aspects of your business.

In the education industry you might see an average multiple of 5x, with a "best in class" multiple as high as 12x. Here are some additional examples of different multiples by industry:

Sector	EBITDA Multiple Range	3 to 5 Year Outlook
Financial	7-12x	Neutral
Food Processing	5-10x	Neutral
Waste & Industrial	4-10x	Positive
Education	5-12x	Neutral
IT & Digital	6-14x	Positive
Energy, Power & Utilities	6-10x	Positive
Transport & Logistics	5-10x	Positive
Healthcare	6-14x	Positive
Tourism	5-12x	Positive
eCommerce	0.75-3x (represents EV/sales)	Positive
Professional Services	5-12x	Positive

Source: Mergermarket

You can control your financial performance in terms of revenue and EBITDA/profit, but you can't control the *multiple range* within your industry. That's set by the capital markets. And keep in mind: When you sell your business, you can't say you're in three or four different markets. You have to choose one.

Taking education as an example, you can see that some businesses have sold for a 5x multiple, while others have sold for a 12x multiple. The difference: How transferable the business is and how well-built the machine is. The more you can demonstrate sustainable and predictable profit growth in your business, the higher you'll climb in your industry range.

Most of my clients start out in the lower to middle end of the range. My goal is to get them to the highest point possible, because that can translate into tens of millions of dollars.

B. WHAT COULD YOUR BUSINESS BE WORTH IN THE FUTURE?

Profit & Value Deltas

Once we arrive at what your business might be worth today, we can discover the differences in profit and value now vs. when you sell your business to private equity. These differences form the *profit delta* and *value delta*.

This can get quite complex so let's simplify as best we can:

Profit Delta:

As profit increases, so does the valuation multiple, but it still remains within the industry range:

Company A = $5M EBITDA x 6x = $30M valuation

Company B = $8M EBITDA x 8x = $64M valuation

The above A and B examples are purely based on the financials. When considering two businesses in the same industry, the more profitable business hits a higher multiple in the industry range.

Then you overlay...

Value Delta:

If two companies have the same profitability, but one is significantly better built and structured, it will achieve a higher overall multiple vs. the other (but still within the industry range):

Company B = $8M EBITDA x 8x = $64M valuation

Company C = $8M EBITDA x 12x = $96M valuation

The second company here (C) is considered "best in class" and gets a multiple kicker vs. other companies based on its strategic value development. Calculating your value delta is the best way to see the financial opportunities you open up by making your business more efficient.

Bringing these two deltas *together* really drives home what your business could be worth once it's fully optimised.

Finally, we want to align this number with your personal *wealth delta*, or as we've called it, your *life-changing number.* Are they similar? Are they far apart? (Of course, taking into account tax post-sale, etc.) How do we bridge the gap?

Discovering these deltas can be an important penny-dropping moment, because now you know what shape the business is in as well its potential. Hopefully, you'll then become inspired to meet your Vivid Vision and achieve your high-value exit.

Intangible Value Drivers

Most of my clients who achieve a high-value exit do so off a *profit* or EBITDA multiple. But that's only part of the game based on a purely financial perspective. Consider this:

*Only **30%–40%** of your company's value is based on the financials.*

*The **other 60%–70%** comes from other areas.*

The good news is that you can control your value, and that starts with strengthening your foundations. You can control the amount of revenue your business generates. You can control the amount of profit or EBITDA your business creates. You can always sell more and spend less. And while you can't control the profit-multiple range in your industry, you *can* influence where you sit on the range, which is going to be the biggest driver of your exit valuation and the wealth your exit creates.

Again, when the profit delta and the value delta are combined, we can *really* maximise the multiple. This is a good example of the art and the science of private equity.

Say you have a poorly structured education business that does $5 million in EBITDA. With the right capital and guidance, you can achieve a low-end 5x multiple and sell it in 3–5 years for $25 million.

Now imagine that your $5 million EBITDA education business is built beautifully, with *intangibles* like solid processes and a great leadership team. When it's time to sell to the PE Sharks, those intangibles drive value and push them to offer a *10x multiplier*. That means you can sell the company for *$50 million,* or *double*.

Once we evaluate your current and desired business valuation, we find the places we can improve. Value is both a science and an art. We look at your value through its finances ("science"), but that still leaves the "art," or 60%–70% from your intangibles.

C. ASSESS YOUR BUSINESS

Strengthening your foundations means knowing where you are today and comparing it to where you want to go. Certain areas to assess, like finances, are obvious. Others, like culture, aren't.

The PE Sharks are going to look at all of it during their due diligence process, so roll up your sleeves and do it in advance. When I work with a business, we conduct our own *shadow due diligence*[60]. We go through a robust assessment, score your business in key areas (see "Worksheets" linked at the end of Part Three) and identify exactly what to fix. It's like ordering an inspection of your house before you put it on the market. Better to learn that you have a damaged roof, ground subsidence or other issues before a buyer's inspector does, and better to fix the problems ahead of time so no one can use them as negotiating tools against you.

Once we know what to fix, we can pave the way for scaling your business.

FIXING ISSUES (DE-RISKING)

We divide our fixable items into key areas (intangible value drivers) that I call ***The 5 Ps***:

1. **People** (structure, hierarchy, culture, succession)
2. **Processes** (documentation, systems, automation)

3. **Proposition** (market, ideal customer, product/service, brand, reputation)
4. **Protection** (IP, risk mitigation, governance, legal/compliance)
5. **Profitability** (overall financial efficiency)

We rank these issues by priority, then implement 90-day sprints to improve each one. Let's go through them individually.

PEOPLE

Which issues in your business are *people*-orientated, including hierarchy, succession planning and culture? *People* covers the quality of the team you build — the leadership team, the management team, and the people above, across and throughout the organization.

Many business owners don't think beyond their leadership team. As I'll talk more about in the Talent-to-Value part of this section, your company's value is driven by the way you build your business around talent in general. Don't just look at the top two layers of your hierarchy; look at key roles *across your organization.* If you have your best people in these positions, then you can align with your growth strategy and reach your life-changing number sooner.

One example: When a *Fortune 500* company analysed thousands of their employees, they identified just 53 who were absolutely crucial to driving their strategy. Some of those roles weren't in leadership. They were analysts further down the organizational chart and technical people focused on innovation.

When you consider your human capital, don't just think about bringing in the next best president, COO or CFO. Those roles are important but consider *all* your talent and resources to find the roles that are going to speed you toward your endgame.

Companies like Apple and Amazon follow this "talent template," but you can and should do it for your small business as well. In a company of 50–100 employees, 5–10 roles might drive the most value. Know what they are, then hire (or re-organize) for them.

Processes

Do you have systems that aren't in place or aren't working? Do you have automation where you need it? Are all your processes documented? Have you considered the impact of AI? *Processes* includes all your standard operating procedures[61] (SOPs), workflows and other elements that help your people work efficiently and effectively.

Establishing SOPs is a vital intangible asset in the eyes of the PE Sharks. They want to see technologies that drive efficiency and create agility and flexibility. SOPs should *more than pay for their cost* by maximizing and optimizing every aspect of your business. By assessing your SOPs, you can eliminate the ones that aren't needed and double down on the ones that are.

Proposition

Your *proposition* might be the market you're in, your product or service, the way you're looking at your offers, or all of these things combined. You might find that you need more customers or rely on too few. And you might discover that your brand and reputation aren't as strong *outside* your walls as they are *inside* them.

I once went into a business that was doing about $40 million in revenue and making $8 million in net profit. The owner wanted to sell his business, and the numbers looked good. The solid EBITDA coupled with an industry multiple between 6 and 10 would have been attractive to the private equity mid-market if it weren't for one glaring problem: The business only had five customers, and two of them accounted for over 50% of its revenues. To make matters worse, those customers were absolutely aligned with and loyal to the founder, and he wanted to transition once he sold the business. For the owner to make a high-value exit, he would have to diversify the customer base and become less important to his customers.

It's a little like having a team with only two star players. They could get injured at any time, and they could follow the coach wherever he goes if he's fired. With that kind of risk, no one wants to buy your company, because it's not *transferable*. It has a massive issue of *market base* or *customer capital*. For private equity to want your business, it must have a range of customers and demographics. If expansion or diversification aren't possible, then you're branded as a "niche business" with a "select market base."

Your *proposition* includes your *brand and culture*. You build a *brand* from the outside-in and a *culture* from the inside-out, but they're two sides of the same coin.

Your *brand* must have meaning. If you develop it in a way that strikes a chord with customers and sets your business apart from its competitors, then it can increase your multiple. Some business owners don't invest in their brand because it doesn't show a direct return on their financials. But it's more complicated than that. In my corporate days, we referred to a strong brand as "a promise of consistency." Like an oven, it warms up — and raises your value — over time.

The same can be said for *culture*. Do you have a positive culture that increases performance, or a toxic one that holds it back? Thanks to various surveys and assessments, you can measure your culture like never before. Think of it as "how people do things when I'm not around." PE wants to know that your team believes in your corporate vision, mission and other elements beyond what they get paid. If you've built an *intentional* culture with solid incentives and rewards, then you can retain the best people in the roles that drive *intangible value* and boost your multiple.

PROTECTION

Protection means legal compliance. It also means protecting assets like IP. If these aren't protected, or loose, then this poses risk, and the valuation will be reduced because of this. Do you have any current or pending lawsuits, or any legal issues that could cause a potential buyer to have problems? If so, how can you mitigate those issues?

PROFITABILITY

This is the last and most important P. *Profitability* is your overall financial efficiency. It includes metrics like profit or EBITDA, as well as other financial performance elements reflected in assessments and statements. Profitability overlaps with your profit and value deltas — what you're worth now and what you plan to be worth in a few years.

Is your business profitable enough for private equity? If not, then it's time to make improvements.

90-DAY SPRINTS

As you start to address the 5Ps, you'll want to rank them by priority and conduct "90-day sprints" on your way to scaling your business. The point of placing a time limit on fixing your business issues is to make sure you do the work. As a business owner, you're likely goal- and deadline-driven. That's why you're successful.

Strengthening your foundations can be a lot of work, but you'll likely realize the benefits right away. I've seen business owners make more money immediately because they're fixing problems, they didn't even know they had. In addition to revenue, they also free up more time for themselves by bringing in the right people and putting them in the right positions. And all the while, they build more value for when they want to sell their business.

Sometimes founders improve their businesses so much that they get to their life-changing number without even having to sell! Sometimes a business owner makes so much more profit from improvements, they can achieve freedom and financial independence without selling their company, which of course is still an exit of sorts.

More commonly, they become much better equipped to close their business deltas and scale from a strong foundation.

BUSINESS ATTRACTIVENESS & EXIT READINESS

Imagine a perfectly built red Ferrari. With its glossy exterior, sleek design and leather seats, it's pristine, orderly, elegant and breathtakingly beautiful. That's how you want private equity to see your business. And as you fix your various issues, you enhance your company's external appearance, or *attractiveness*, to those outside investors. Tools to make a business appealing include creative advertising, savvy public relations and social media campaign(s) and building an iconic brand.

But let's say our Ferrari only *appears* attractive, and we find it has mechanical and other issues under the hood. While *business attractiveness* goes from the outside in *exit readiness* is determined from the inside out. *Exit readiness* is how you build that engine and fix those brakes, so your business becomes safer and performs better. If someone looks at your car and opens the bonnet, you want them to see that the engine is perfectly tuned and working, mechanical aspects are spotless, and the inner workings are as attractive as the exterior.

Strengthening foundations is at its core exit readiness + business attractiveness. It's making sure your business looks attractive from the outside and works beautifully inside. Once your business foundations are optimized and in place, you can use what I call *advanced scale strategies* to accelerate your performance and increase profits and overall value.

TALENT-TO-VALUE

When I worked at Getty Images, we acquired a lot of companies. As we've discussed, rapid growth is achieved through the five levers of value expansion. But here's the thing: Underneath that value expansion is *talent,* the people who put in the work to ensure that value is always being created and expanded.

It doesn't matter if a PE firm acquires all the right businesses to drive their value and profitability. If they don't know how to integrate those businesses and consolidate their value into one entity or group, they'll run into massive trouble. Getty Images had a small team led by our Head of Integrations who made sure that the businesses we acquired were mapped neatly with the rest of the organization. Making sure that the people and culture pieces all worked together smoothly was a highly strategic job.

Did our Head of Integrations sit on the Getty board? No. It wasn't a C-suite role. It wasn't even at the VP or director level. Yet despite the fact that it was a department head position, or what we'd call "mid-level management," our executives spent a lot of time choosing the right person for it. They understood how critical the role was, and they knew they needed the right person in that seat.

Without such wisdom, many business owners and entrepreneurs try to grow and scale their companies by first addressing their leadership and hierarchy. They start by filling senior leadership roles like CEO, CFO and COO. They assume that the fastest route to growth and value creation is letting those leaders build their own teams.

What private equity does differently — and what we did so well at Getty — is *map talent-to-value*[62]. This concept was created by Sandy Ogg, who worked at Unilever and Blackstone. It means looking across your entire organization to identify the roles that create the most value, then putting the right talent in those places.

The best people aren't always in the top two layers of your business. Sometimes you need particularly talented people much further down in the organization, especially in critical technical positions that add as much (if not more) value than senior leadership roles.

Let's talk about the four things PE firms do to make "talent-to-value" work in their favour:

1. UNDERSTAND HOW TO CREATE VALUE

PE is the best value-creation machine on the planet. Day-in, day-out, private equity investors consider strategies that deliver shareholder value. To optimize your talent, deliver on your strategy, boost your value and attract the PE Sharks, be clear on a few things:

- How does your business create value?
- What drives that value today?
- How can you create *more* of that value?
- What resources do you need to ensure that value creation actually happens?

2. Identify the Most Important Roles Around that Value

Once you understand how value is created in your business, identify the roles that most drive that value. But beware two pitfalls: ***defining critical roles in terms of hierarchy*** and ***regarding roles and talent as interchangeable.***

In other words, just because someone's in a higher salary band doesn't mean they're creating more value than someone a few rungs down. It's the roles that matter — the ones that create, enable and protect value in your business. What are the *roles* — not the talent — that drive the most value for you and your stakeholders?

3. Get the Right Talent into the Right Roles

Once you've listed your company's critical roles, it's about getting the right talent into them. This is another task that PE does better than anybody. Lots of organizations struggle to make unbiased decisions in placing certain people in certain roles because they don't have enough knowledge or data about their people. If you've struggled with employees who didn't work out in the roles they were hired for or promoted to, then you know you've got your work cut out for you. Make it a habit to assess talent against the specific needs of each role in your business and the outcomes that need to be delivered by those roles.

If you *don't* have the right people for these roles, then you need a strategy to recruit new talent while developing existing talent. That includes building a succession pipeline so critical roles are never left unoccupied. Some business owners lag behind PE firms in scaling their businesses because they fill critical roles with long-time loyalists. Assessing talent objectively means sometimes hiring from outside the organization.

In private equity, it's not uncommon to rotate people around in various roles just to map the perfect talent-to-value mix — even at the leadership level. That's why you frequently hear about these big companies changing CEOs and CFOs multiple times in a single year. PE isn't afraid to make "heavy-handed" changes throughout a business, so long as those changes create value.

4. MANAGE PERFORMANCE AND DEVELOP TALENT IN REAL TIME

A select few businesses succeed at hiring, onboarding and promoting great talent in their companies. Some even put the best people in their most critical, value-creating roles. But many fall short when it comes to *managing these people's performance* and developing their talents in real-time.

Larger corporations typically conduct employee performance reviews only a couple times a year, which makes it hard to assess performance or make personnel changes. Private equity firms, on the other hand, compress value-creation time because they need the agility to make personnel and organizational changes fast. That's why you'll never find a PE firm doing performance assessments just once or twice a year.

I once took the stage after a prominent sales trainer and speaker named Jack Daly (jackdalysales.com). In his talk, he said, "Most sports teams are run better than most businesses." His rationale:

- They put the right people in the right roles. If you're a great striker[63], you're not going to be put on defence!
- They practice. There's a culture of training and improvement.
- Performance coaching happens continually in real time. Players always receive feedback on their performance so they can improve it.

Active evolution through *active* management is an interesting way to look at talent development. That's how PE firms manage their businesses. They *sweat the asset*. People are usually the costliest asset in a business, so they deserve to be actively and intelligently managed like any successful sports team.

Getty had thousands of employees when I was there. As you can imagine, assessing that talent and managing their performance in real-time wasn't easy. So, we identified 85 absolutely critical roles throughout the organization that generated the company's current and future value. Those people were then assessed weekly, or even daily. We closely monitored their KPIs and OKRs[64]. We sat on weekly scrums[65] with them to see if they were on track with their tasks. If anyone in those roles failed to perform within expectations, we rotated them so we could better map our talent to the value we needed to create.

We did this over a two-year timeframe. The result: a massive increase in EBITDA and an impressive reduction in operating costs. It also clarified our culture: Our people would get things done at a high level, with maximum operational precision.

All this talk about mapping talent-to-value and creating operational precision doesn't apply to my business, you might be thinking. *We don't have thousands of people.* It doesn't matter. Even if you have 50 or fewer employees, you can find the 5 or 10 who make the biggest difference in your business. It's the same idea.

Having highly talented people in your business isn't enough. What matters is making sure they're in the right roles. When you do that, your business can become extremely valuable to a sophisticated buyer and give you a high-value exit that leads to financial and personal freedom.

ENTREPRENEURIAL OPERATING SYSTEM™ (EOS)

The *Entrepreneurial Operating System™* (EOS) is a way of simplifying and improving the key operations in a business. When I was doing turnarounds and scaling companies in my private equity days, we would often use EOS as the key framework to simplify and scale operations. I thoroughly recommend reading Gino Wickham's book, *Traction,* and his book, *Rocket Fuel* as additional reading to support the principles in this book.

https://www.eosworldwide.com/

STEP 3: Growth: Scale Fast & Expand Value

After building the right foundations for your business and installing your intangible value drivers, it's time to think more strategically and expansively. This chapter will show you how to do exactly that by growing fast and building value. We'll dive into the art of scaling to uncover the secrets that PE firms don't want you to know.

Remember: You can't scale a business on its foundation alone. For the scaling strategies I cover in this section, you need fluency in other growth types. Let's dive deeper into *organic growth, strategic growth* and *exponential growth.*

ORGANIC GROWTH

Many owners think the only way to grow their business is by onboarding one customer at a time. That's *organic* growth (OG). Although it's important, it tends to be slow, expensive and vulnerable to market changes, economic downturns and other external factors. Relying solely on OG means throwing significant marketing resources at your business that may not always yield the desired results.

To be fair, OG *can* be effective by itself. But anyone who has bought Google Ads or Facebook Ads knows how slow and expensive it can be. As you place and test ads, you often burn through money on sales and marketing without seeing the results you need.

Enter the external risks. Case in point: COVID-19 pandemic lockdowns led to major inflation and economic volatility, moving many businesses toward digital transactions and e-commerce. Unless you're 100% prepared for major changes like that, you're subjecting your business to unnecessary risk unless you also target *strategic growth* (SG).

TWO TYPES OF MARKETING

Remember that only two types of marketing exist, and both pertain only to organic growth:

1. **Brand Marketing**: This is the emotional connection customers feel with your business. What attributes do they

associate with your company, and do they perceive your values and goals as similar to theirs? A *brand* is a promise of consistency. Creating a strong brand over the long run creates value for your business, but it doesn't solve the immediate problem of sales. Like an oven, it takes a while to heat up, but it stays hot and warm for a long time.

2. **Direct Response Marketing**: This is the microwave. Your food is hot in 30 seconds, but that heat can be short-lived. *Direct response* is leads, funnels, promotions, determining the exact right offer — all the activity you undertake to pull in and convert customers.

Focus too much on brand, and your business won't grow enough *now* to be sustainable. Focus too much on direct response, and you'll enjoy growth today without building *long-term* connections or loyalty. To build a foundation for *strategic growth*, you have to do both.

Strategic Growth

Unlike organic growth, strategic growth can scale your business much faster through its compounding nature. It includes leveraging networks, partnerships and joint ventures (JV), mergers and acquisitions (M&A), and accessing and Structuring Capital.

Strategic growth powers you to rapidly expand your customer base, access new markets and leverage existing resources and assets — all of which accelerates your value.

ORGANIC VS. STRATEGIC GROWTH

In addition to what we discussed in Part Two, Lever #1: Revenue Growth, my mentor Jay Abraham identifies three ways to grow a business organically:

1. Increase the number of customers.
2. Increase purchase frequency (repeat purchases, etc).
3. Increase the average transaction value (bundling, cross-selling, pricing etc.).

Keeping a customer is far more efficient and less costly than *finding* one. The Holy Grail for private equity is *lifetime value (LTV)*: customers who keep buying your product or service as long as possible and also increase their spending over time. Recurring income is both valuable and transferable. If you can show that your business not only finds and keeps customers (the first half of *lifetime value*), but also *increases customer spending,* then PE firms will fall over themselves vying for your business.

How else is SG different from OG? If the goal is #1 (increase your number of customers), an organic approach might involve doing more marketing, while a strategic growth approach might be buying one of your competitors and absorbing *their* customers.

Most business owners know OG but not SG. Combining the two opens the doors to EG, or *exponential growth* — the "compound interest" effect that compresses time and accelerates scale, which the PE Sharks have mastered.

EXPONENTIAL GROWTH

Implementing organic and strategic growth tactics in tandem can 10x your business, thus the "exponential." For example, say you're organically growing your business 20% year-on-year with Facebook Ads. While that's happening, you're also looking into potential partnerships and acquisitions — usually competitors or suppliers up or downstream. The goal is to build an ecosystem of businesses that can serve the market in a bigger and more intentional way.

All of this requires capital, so you might have to leverage some debt, put more money into proven marketing techniques and make capital available for acquisitions, as well as look into joint ventures and partnerships. If you can do this as part of a comprehensive growth strategy, then you'll drive exponential growth.

Why do PE firms so often buy up everything in the space and create a bigger entity? Because the bigger the entity, the less the risk and the higher the overall valuation.

But it can't happen without a solid foundation. My clients can get frustrated because we spend so much time kicking the tires on these value drivers. But if they start buying businesses before they solve a brand reputation problem or define their culture, then they're just going to add complexity and problems before inevitably going back to fix their foundations.

Driving revenue and cutting costs is important, but it's only part of the equation. Leveraging capital, networks and relationships complete it. As a business owner, it's time to break free from the limitations of organic-only growth and embrace strategic growth to achieve exponential growth.

Remember this equation:

$$OG + SG = EG^{10}$$

Where organic growth combined with strategic growth equals exponential growth to the power of ten.

How is this like *compound interest*?

See the graph below:

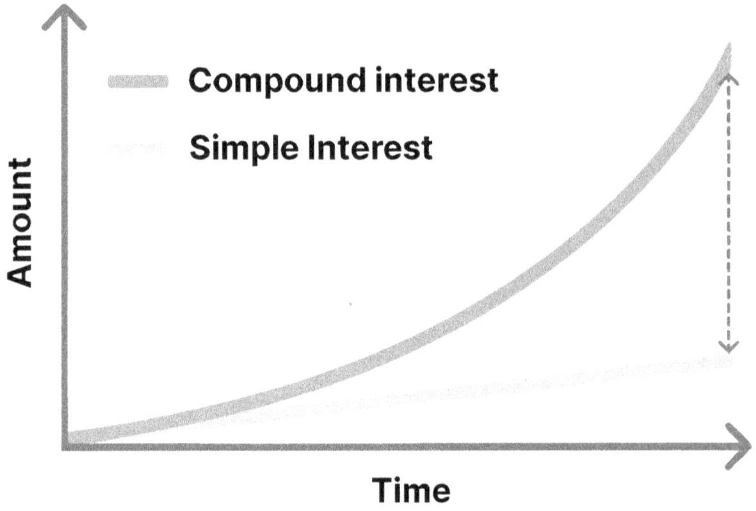

STRATEGIC GROWTH STRATEGIES

A. THE POWER OF LEVERAGE

[66]

I used to work for publishing giant East Midlands Allied Press (EMAP). At the time, EMAP had organic growth, joint ventures and a few small acquisitions under its belt, but something was missing. During the tumultuous times of 2007–2008 — just before the big financial crash — EMAP struggled to drive shareholder value and faced the possibility of a sale or breakup. Eventually, it was split into two operating companies and sold to private equity and a private independent media group. My challenge was to restructure the business before the breakup, which involved making tough decisions like laying off employees. It was considered a successful move, but it left a bitter taste in my mouth.

Shortly after this, I joined Getty Images, a company that had recently been acquired by a PE firm called Hellman and Friedman[67].

Here's where I realised what was missing from EMAP's business strategy. Getty had a clear growth strategy with mergers and acquisitions at its core. On my first day, I was told that the company didn't rely as much on organic growth. My job would be to help them find more companies to acquire on top of the many they already owned.

After comparing the painstaking experience of growing a business one customer at a time vs. scaling fast through M&A, I couldn't imagine a world where M&A didn't sit at the heart of growth. That experience propelled me into private equity, where I gained a deeper understanding of leveraging acquisitions, joint ventures and partnerships.

Private equity leverages both *capital* and *networks*. You may already be familiar with the idea of leveraging capital, but you also need to harness the power of networks and the relationships they create. PE firms have these skills in droves because they're the most important concepts in building value, scaling fast, unlocking opportunities and maximizing resources.

To apply these principles to your own business, start with a strategic partnership or a joint venture with a supplier, competitor or other entity that has a product, service or asset you need. This initial collaboration can eventually evolve into a more permanent arrangement, such as a merger or an acquisition.

B. Partnerships & Joint Ventures (JV)

The most basic tool of strategic growth, a **partnership** can be two businesses that go about working *together* in some aspect of what they do. Essentially, you look for entities that can help you leverage assets like products, geography or audience.

You might start a *supplier partnership* in which you share data. In a more traditional partnership, you might find a company that sells something to your target audience, then work out a way to communicate your offer to their customers in exchange for money or another asset. In traditional marketing, you pay up front to reach an audience. With this type of partnership, you pay for success after the fact (sometimes called *performance marketing*). Or you go on stage and make your offer at a partner's event, maybe paying a fee to go on stage or paying 20% of all sales made.

These are examples of strategic growth because the partner entity has already invested in building the assets you're accessing. You're going into the slipstream of the work they've done.

Partnerships are one of my favourite ways to grow a business because you generally don't have to invest a lot of money up front, and you gain on the outcome. If you've been focusing on organic growth and want to test the waters on strategic growth, set up a few partnerships. If you want to go a step further, explore a *joint venture.*

A **joint venture** typically occurs when two entities pool their resources to create a new 50/50 legal structure *for a specific purpose*. It could be a fresh venture, a collaborative campaign or even a completely new company. The point is that both parties contribute roughly equal resources to it.

"A joint venture (JV) is a business arrangement in which two or more parties agree to pool their resources for the purpose of accomplishing a specific task. This task can be a new project or any other business activity. Each of the participants in a joint venture is responsible for profits, losses, and costs associated with it. However, the venture is its own entity, separate from the participants' other business interests."

—https://www.investopedia.com/terms/j/jointventure.asp

C. MERGERS & ACQUISITIONS (M&A)

Bigger than simply combining resources for a specific opportunity (partnership), but similar to an entity created for a specific purpose (joint venture), a **merger** involves businesses bringing their whole companies together to create a new entity.

> "A merger is an agreement that unites two existing companies into one new company. There are several types of mergers and reasons companies complete mergers. Mergers and acquisitions (M&A) are commonly done to expand a company's reach, expand into new segments, or gain market share. All of these are done to increase shareholder value. Often, during a merger, companies have a no-shop clause to prevent purchases or mergers by additional companies."
>
> —https://www.investopedia.com/terms/m/merger.asp

In many cases, mergers involve a 50/50 or 60/40 ownership split. The companies involved believe they can create more value and mitigate market risks more effectively together than alone. Mergers become especially popular when fast-growing markets or inherent risks prompt businesses to consolidate. Scale becomes vital because a larger presence delivers stronger negotiating power and shared resources. As previously mentioned, bigger businesses also often command higher valuations because they own more resources and are seen as less risky.

An **acquisition** occurs when one company or entity takes over another by purchasing the majority of its shares or other assets. The goal is to assimilate or absorb the acquired entity into the buyer's existing structure. Sometimes the acquired company becomes part of a larger group. For instance, when I was part of Ascend Learning, our group comprised several acquisitions bought together. Each of these businesses had its own brands, and profit and loss statements. But all financial performance and resources were shared within the group. As a private, equity-backed organization, Ascend Learning owned all these businesses.

Mergers and acquisitions have transformative potential that can catapult your business to new heights. When we look at successful companies like Apple, Google, and Amazon, we often overlook the fact that acquisitions are a crucial aspect of their growth strategies. These giants acquire other businesses so discreetly that we hardly ever hear about it.

Over the past five years, Apple alone has made more than 100 acquisitions. They weren't so much about chasing growth, expanding offerings or boosting market share as they were about acquiring the *right talent* to fuel future success and keep shareholders happy. (Conveniently, they also neutralized competitors and other potential threats.)

Loads of mid-market and lower mid-market businesses don't know the power of scaling through M&A. That's a tragedy, because they're sitting on so much untapped potential. With enterprise values ranging from $20 million to $150 million, these owners are missing out on an incredible opportunity to skyrocket their growth.

Mergers and acquisitions can be *horizontal* or *vertical.* If you're a U.K. business looking to enter the U.S. market, you'll need to buy assets and businesses that are already there. That's horizontal. But you might also buy the means of production or retail outlets that sell your goods. That's vertical. But let's define these even a bit better:

- *Horizontal* is buying another business in your current industry, like a competitor.
- *Vertical* is buying another business up or down your supply chain, like a car manufacturer buying a dealer network or vehicle servicing company.

Rollups

Acquisitions are the first part of a two-part strategy to scale fast and build value. The other part is the *rollup*. It's not enough to simply acquire one business after the other and leave things at that. That's like buying car parts without building the car. To boost your business value, you have to leverage the strengths of each acquired company into an entity greater than the sum of its parts. PE firms do this through the *roll-up*, also called the *buy-and-build* approach.

Here's how it works:

- You identify a target company in your sector you want to purchase.

- Instead of running it as a standalone entity, you combine its operations with your established business and capitalize on your management systems, back-office functions and infrastructure.

- This reduces costs and optimizes resources, making the whole greater than the sum of its parts.

See the magic? This strategy accelerates your growth and value creation. That's why it's the jewel in the PE crown. And right now, PE firms see a golden opportunity in baby boomers who've built successful businesses and are looking to retire. By offering these aging entrepreneurs a fair deal, they can acquire their businesses while also gaining access to their valuable customer bases, relationships and brand equity.

When you master the *buy-and-build* strategy, you unlock tremendous value and supercharge your growth. By acquiring businesses at favourable prices and integrating them into your operations, you can compress time. It's like turbocharging your business engine. Suddenly, you're scaling up faster, capitalizing on synergies and realizing the full potential of the assets you've acquired.

D. ACCESSING & STRUCTURING CAPITAL

Just as you can renovate your house either by borrowing money or taking out a home equity loan, a business can access capital by taking on debt. This step can be placed earlier or later in the process.

Finding Money Already in Your Business

1. Look over your organization's current use of available money and determine if it's the best use of those funds.

2. Identify inefficiencies in your current capital use. Maybe several processes can be improved at the same time.

3. Make reallocations on your balance sheet to fund your growth strategy investments.

Securing Funds from External Sources

Even after doing the above, you might find gaps in needed capital. In these cases, private equity will raise debt to facilitate strategic growth, often by leveraging assets on the balance sheet. For example, you can often raise 70% – 80% against receivables (in the future) to access cash now. You might have balance sheet assets like plants or machinery that you can raise funds against.

Rather than buying a company outright, private equity usually buys a majority of its shares instead. In fact, today it often makes *growth equity investments,* where it puts a small amount of capital into a business to fuel its growth, then see how it responds. It's like a small bet to test the waters before going "all-in." A PE firm might also obtain first right of refusal on an acquisition as part of that process.

SCALE MATTERS

Whether it's joint ventures, mergers or acquisitions, these high-level opportunities offer tremendous power and potential for business owners like you. By allowing you to combine your strengths, leverage pooled resources and create a more valuable and less risky entity, they can make you more competitive, more powerful at the negotiating table, and more likely to achieve a high-value exit. It's not an exaggeration to say that these partnerships can reshape entire industries and open doors to new opportunities that otherwise might have been difficult to access.

In the Scale To Sale™ Methodology, we're not interested in individual campaigns or one-off projects. Our focus is on helping you achieve strategic growth. We want you to grow your company as quickly as possible. The best way to do that is to acquire other businesses and their assets.

If you want to build value and scale quickly, acquisitions should be on your radar. But one piece of advice: Don't rush into one. If you're just starting out or making less than a million in revenue (EBITDA), focus on organic growth first. Once you cross the million-dollar-revenue mark and head toward $1 million in EBITDA, consider both organic and strategic growth. And definitely consider acquisitions.

That said, you can become much more appealing to private equity if you push your profit to +$5 million. At that level, you could become their first platform acquisition. They'll use your business as a launchpad to acquire more, and that's a valuable position for a founder to be in.

So, if you're at that million-dollar revenue mark, start thinking about acquisitions. In the meantime, set your intention to scale to an EBITDA milestone that will catch the attention of PE firms. This goal alone dramatically increases your ability to realize a high-value exit on your terms.

STEP 4:
PREPARE & PROFIT UP

The fourth step in the Scale To Sale™ Methodology is *profiting up*. This is where you organize the logistics of your high-value exit to ensure you receive the maximum valuation from prospective buyers.

A proper exit strategy requires careful planning and execution *well in advance of going to market*. Many business owners make the mistake of doing all these preparations at the *same time* they initiate the sales process. They spruce their business up superficially, like applying lipstick to a pig, forgetting that they're dealing with sophisticated buyers who can see that it's still a pig.

Don't make that mistake. This flawed approach is precisely why many so-called "business experts" fail to achieve their desired results. To achieve a true high-value exit, start the exit and value expansion process long before you consider going to market.

Going back to our house analogy, *prepare and profit up* is like the post-renovations phase. Before you sell a house, you fix its issues (Step 2). After that, you might decide you want to make it bigger by adding an extension or loft conversion (Step 3). Your house will look messy with scaffolding and tools everywhere, but it'll be a more valuable asset once it has an extension and other improvements. *Prepare and Profit Up* (Step 4) is the clean-up and staging process after the renovation. You remove the scaffolding, clean the rooms, clear the rubbish out of the garden and generally make your house as pretty as possible so a buyer feels emotionally attached to it. Going back to our previous metaphor, you haven't just put lipstick on a pig; you've created a prize horse.

Once we've gotten your business to the high valuation we want to exit for, we need to consolidate everything and tighten up your financials. This is where you build your advisory team and conduct shadow due diligence. "Due diligence" is also part of Step 2, but only to show us what needs fixing. There, we expect a low score. Here, the score should be as high as possible.

The *Prepare and Profit Up* process might take six months, but it's worth it. You don't want to put your business on the market until you're confident it'll earn the number you want. I call this second assessment our "last sense check" to make sure all your key value drivers are in place.

Simulate a potential buyer's process by hiring a third-party to thoroughly examine your business and create a data room. Identify red flags and concerns that could arise during the actual sales process. And address them beforehand to ensure a smooth transaction.

Keep in mind: These due diligence processes are *ours.* Your potential buyers will run their own assessments during the sales process. Like a political campaign that conducts opposition research on its own candidate before its opponent does the same thing, the goal is to minimize issues ahead of time, know what to expect and minimize surprises.

You need at least 12 months to prepare for an exit, but the most successful entrepreneurs allow up to 36 months to complete Steps 1 through 4. (Sometimes a business owner comes to me with everything in place, allowing us to go straight to Step 4 and cut the timeline down a couple years, but Step 4 alone can take 6 months.) So, it generally takes 12–36 months to get your business ready, then the sale itself can take 6-12 months. This extended timeframe allows you to prepare, make strategic decisions and implement growth initiatives to elevate your business value. The timeframe depends on how far away you are from your life-changing number when we start. But by investing time and effort into these early stages, you set yourself up for a truly lucrative, life-changing event.

Many business owners get stuck in Step 4 because they fail to recognize the significance of proper planning and long-term preparation. But not you. Because you're reading this chapter, you'll gain a deeper understanding of what it truly takes to achieve a high-value exit.

In the next few pages, we'll explore the critical components of preparing for a successful exit. Even if you're not 100% ready to put your company on the market, don't skip this chapter. While the journey to selling your business is an emotional one, it's also filled with logical considerations. The earlier you start these preparations, the better.

LOOK AT YOUR FINANCIALS

While intangible assets can make up 60% to your company's market value to private equity, financial stability comprises a crucial 40%. In other words, you need rock-solid, *audit-ready* financials to really engage the PE Sharks. As the saying goes, "Time kills all deals." You don't want to waste time dealing with financial inconsistencies when you could be closing a fast and advantageous deal. The cleaner your books, the smoother the sale process. Simple as that.

First, you need to overcome a common temptation among entrepreneurs: *value attribution bias*[68]. Business owners tend to look at their own work through rose-coloured glasses. Their optimism is their greatest asset, but it can also breed denial.

That's why you should seek external expertise from a highly skilled CFO[69] (full-time or fractional). You may already have a talented CFO on board, but an external expert with private equity experience can bring a fresh perspective, as he or she identifies adjustments that can impact your net profit. Known as *add backs*[70], these adjustments account for exceptional expenses or investments outside your regular operations. Incorporating them usually raises your EBITDA to a more favourable number, plus when combined with the multiple of EBITDA, it can significantly boost your valuation. Remember this — any adjusted or normalized EBITDA is multiplied by your valuation multiple. So, every $100k of EBITDA added back could be worth 5x or 10x that amount when the business is sold.

I also advise getting a *Quality of Earnings* report done by an external party, commonly referred to as a "Q of E." A Q of E report provides the foundation for your eventual buyer's offer, and they typically conduct one during due diligence to assess your historical and potential revenues and profits. By conducting *your own* Q of E in advance — with the assistance of an external expert who specializes in transactional due diligence — you can identify hidden flaws and discrepancies in your financials, clear skeletons from your closet and prepare yourself for any potential buyer's challenging questions

Preparing your own commissioned Q of E also carries symbolic weight. Buyers see your proactive approach, readiness to engage in serious discussions and willingness to go *beyond* their expectations. By highlighting your meticulousness and commitment to financial excellence, it reshapes the conversation, demonstrates your readiness to sell and accelerates the process. You are seen as the prize vs. the prey.

This brings up an important, even bigger point: Because PE buyers are attracted to entrepreneurs who can make sound financial decisions and generate consistent profits, you need to manage the *psychology* of your high-value exit. The more confident a PE firm feels about your financial stability, the stronger their emotional attachment will grow. The more they see impeccable financials complemented by exceptional intangible assets, the higher their offer will be. Getting your financial house in order instils a sense of confidence and competence. You exude an aura of professionalism and reliability. They see you as one of them, which is a powerful position to be in.

On a more practical level, a comprehensive understanding of your adjusted EBITDA and its potential value empowers you to sit across the table from a PE Shark from a position of strength — the *prize*, not the prey. You can confidently present the financial data that highlights your true profitability and potential.

Don't sit at that table alone. Surround yourself with experts who can guide you through the emotional and strategic aspects of the process. Seek the advice of experienced CFOs, transactional due diligence specialists, and experienced consultants who've navigated similar paths.

Decide If You're Staying or Going

In addition to addressing your financials, ask yourself the big question posed by The Clash in 1982: "After I sell my business, will I stay, or will I go?" Hopefully you've thought about this from day one of your exit planning journey, but it becomes pressing in the 6–12 months before you put your business up for sale. During this time, you need absolute clarity on your future role in the company, as well as your succession plan.

Yes, you still need to demonstrate to potential buyers that your business can thrive without you. But if you wait too long to make the decision on staying or leaving, you risk not having the right team in place to ensure a smooth transition to whomever buys your business.

The Six-Week Test

Have you created the kind of "transferrable asset" that private equity wants? You'll know your business doesn't depend too much on you when you can take a six-week vacation, confident that core activities will be handled, and payroll will be met. You can check in with senior leadership mid-way through but stay away from day-to-day operations. If your business doesn't run like it's supposed to, then you'll know what work remains to be done.

The decision to stay or go can be personal or pragmatic. Some entrepreneurs choose to stay with their business even after selling it, because they find it hard to let go emotionally. Others opt to roll over their equity and invest in the newly formed entity. With support and investment from a PE firm, they aim to scale the business even further before pursuing another exit strategy — like taking a second bite of the apple.

If you do decide to leave your company, have a competent number two in place. For example, employ a president and promote them to CEO during the Profit Up or sooner. This will allow you to step back from day-to-day operations and take on a more strategic role — say, as chairperson — while remaining a significant investor.

This sounds easier than it is. Many business owners wrestle emotionally with the decision to stay or leave until the last possible minute. I understand that completely, but I can also tell you this:

The number one reason why PE transactions fall apart or never materialize is that a business owner gets cold feet.

I've seen it too many times. An owner's identity is so intertwined with their business that they grow unsure and anxious about what to do next. They withdraw from the process and leave a life-changing sum of money on the table.

Take the time to reflect on your personal goals, aspirations and desires. Seek the advice of mentors, fellow entrepreneurs and trusted advisors who've been through similar situations. Think seriously about your legacy. Your personal goals and values will guide you toward a choice that will deliver the success and sense of purpose you want and deserve.

ALIGN YOUR *FIVE PS*

The Prepare and Profit Up phase is where you align your previous work to prepare for your high-value exit. That means aligning the ***Five Ps*** we covered previously:

1. **People** (structure, hierarchy, culture, succession)
2. **Processes** (documentation, systems, automation)
3. **Proposition** (market, ideal customer, product/service, brand, reputation)
4. **Protection** (IP, risk mitigation, governance, legal/compliance)
5. **Profitability** (overall financial efficiency)

Aligning the Five Ps is about fusing the elements that contribute to your company's value. Aligning *human capital* (your employees' skills, knowledge and expertise) with *structural capital* (the systems, processes and intellectual property that drive efficiency and innovation), creates a solid foundation for growth. Aligning *customer capital* (customer relationships, loyalty and trust) with *social capital* (your brand reputation and network of connections) further amplifies your value and market position.

These five capitals hold the key to unlocking exponential growth and attracting buyers who will offer you premium valuations for your business. That's because a well-aligned spectrum of your Five Ps allows you to create two important things:

1. Your growth (exit) story
2. Your win themes.

Let's dive into these two areas.

WRITE YOUR COMPELLING GROWTH STORY

A *compelling growth story* showcases your company's value to buyers who are betting on its future success. Going beyond highlighting past achievements, it focuses on the growth trajectory that makes your business an attractive investment opportunity. You'll want to show that you've built something great that has withstood challenges and will continue to show resilience.

The reason I also call this "your exit story" is the quality of what you produce here defines both the certainty of your exit and the price someone will pay for your business. It demonstrates growth, which equals higher value which equals a better overall outcome for you.

Closely related to this are your *win themes*.

Identify Your Win Themes

Popularised by author Jim Collins, the *flywheel effect* refers to a series of interconnected initiatives that generate momentum and produce superior results when set in motion. For example, an energy company might distinguish itself by creating a strong organizational culture. This improves sales channel relationships, which then improves lead volume and quality. The result is more customers, higher profitability and greater efficiency through refined systems and processes. A focus on exceptional customer experience then further enhances the company's relationships with sales channels, thus completing the flywheel cycle.

In this example, the company's decision to leveraging its people and culture is what I call its *win theme.* It was the critical strategic decision that enabled the business to stand out from its competitors, and it'll justify a premium valuation from a PE buyer should the owner put it up for sale.

To develop your win themes, start with your growth story. Identify three unique qualities that distinguish you from your competition. Then draw a complete flywheel cycle from those qualities to develop comprehensive win themes for your business.

But don't stop there.

As you navigate the process of taking your business to market, storytelling becomes a crucial element. To reinforce your position at the highest valuation range, consistently communicate your growth story and win themes in all buyer interactions. Once you've identified these win themes, consistently use them in presentations, dialogues and narratives to help potential buyers envision your company's future success and value.

Also align your list of *growth strategies*. Remember when we talked about organic growth, margin expansion, acquiring other businesses and bolting them together with yours? If you're increasing your prices or positively influencing your customers' buying habits, bring that into your growth story. If you're looking at improving your profit margins through automation, bring that in as well. The goal is to show how your business has become more valuable through the initiatives you've started to deploy and how these initiatives keep producing value in the future.

If you're doing a buy-and-build strategy, your growth story and win themes should reflect that. Private equity looks for businesses that can serve as platforms for future acquisitions or integrate seamlessly into their existing platform. When you conduct thorough competitor analyses and identify potential acquisition targets, your business becomes extremely attractive to PE. They love the prospect of acquiring additional businesses immediately after yours, because it creates a flywheel effect for *them*: You streamline their processes, save them time and effort, and enable them to execute their long-term plan more swiftly — all of which enhances their reputation with investors.

SIMPLIFY YOUR STRATEGY

Despite everything I've thrown at you in this Scale To Sale™ Methodology step, it's now time to *simplify* your strategy and streamline your approach. While you've been diligently building your growth story, it's equally important to create a simple business plan, or what I call a *one-page strategy*. In the midst of rapid growth, numerous moving parts can make it challenging to navigate the intricacies of the business and the broader market landscape. In other words, you don't want to be in the thick of growing and scaling your business while tons of other things swirl around you.

Great leaders work in the weeds of their business while also looking at the big picture. But moving between these two perspectives can be jarring. That's why simplicity is key. As an external advisor focused on maximizing value and positioning businesses for an exit, my role often involves chipping away at complexities to present the most concise model possible. This simplified business plan becomes the foundation of the business's sales pitch when it goes to market.

Being in private equity is like being in the NBA. If you're there at all, you're better than 99.9% of the population at what you do. But being among the most sophisticated people in your field doesn't necessarily mean that you like complexity. PE Sharks are sophisticated buyers, but they crave clarity and love simple businesses. So rather than succumb to the temptation to make your business seem complex to impress a PE buyer, do the opposite.

PE investors may be enthusiastic about acquiring your business, but they may not understand your specific market in depth. To be frank, they don't need to. They just need a clear understanding of how you've created value and intend to sustain it. Now is the time to channel the spirit of Leonardo da Vinci, who famously chipped away at stone to reveal his remarkable statues. A clear and concise narrative will resonate with buyers, help them quickly grasp the value you've created and get them excited about opportunities ahead.

DIFFERENTIATE YOUR VALUE PROPOSITION

Let's draw some inspiration from Seth Godin's book *Purple Cow*: Imagine you're driving down a road and all you see are brown cows grazing in the fields. Nothing catches your eye because brown cows are everywhere. But amidst this sea of brown cows, you spot a purple one. That sight would be so remarkable, you might crash your car. At the very least, you'd stop and go, "What is that?!"

Human beings are drawn to the unique, which is why crafting a *differentiated value proposition* for your business is so important. Remember those *win themes* we discussed? It's time to bring them together and identify what makes your business the purple cow in your industry.

A *differentiated value proposition* is so important because it can vault your business to the top of your industry's valuation range. If that range falls between 8 and 15 times EBITDA and your business is just another brown cow with low transferable value and messy financials, then PE will either put you at the low end of the range or walk away completely.

If, on the other hand, you've pulled all the elements together, crafted a great story, assembled an exceptional team, know your unique selling points compared to your competitors, and *developed a compelling value proposition*, then you're a purple cow worth 15 times EBITDA. After all, who wouldn't pay extra for a purple cow?

What's the difference between a weak value proposition and a strong one?

Weak:

"We provide cost-effective car insurance for everyone."

Strong:

"Fifteen minutes could save you 15% or more on car insurance."

Recognize the second one? If you do, it's because GEICO has drilled it in your head. It's a strong value proposition because it's hard-hitting, specific and unique in the highly "brown cow" car insurance industry.

Finally, let's bring this step home with the last part of profiting up your business: building your *advisory team.*

BUILD YOUR ADVISORY TEAM

I typically start working with a business 12–36 months before its planned exit, the latter being more common. During this period, I assist in building an advisory team to guide a successful sale. While many owners choose me specifically for this reason, others struggle with the idea of bringing in advisors or consultants. My response: *We're dealing with the biggest financial transaction of your life, selling what you've built for potentially eight or nine figures. You can't do it alone. You need an army of experts and special forces to support you.*

Consider having an advisor on your board early on who can help with your exit plan. Your actual exit may seem far off but remember to reverse engineer your desired outcome. As you progress, you'll find *three key roles* to fill:

ROLE #1: PERSONAL TAX ADVISOR/ WEALTH ADVISOR

Prioritize this immediately. If you leave tax mitigation considerations until the later stages, you might find yourself caught off-guard when you least expect it. A wealth manager or financial advisor can work with you to understand your assets, desired exit number and investment strategies. Neglect these roles, and you could lose millions in tax savings. Fill them early, and you'll have the right processes and structures in place to maximize your capital event.

Know the difference between a personal wealth manager/tax advisor and the accountant who handles your business numbers. They can be the same person, or they can be separate. In some cases — especially if you have business partners — it's beneficial to have a personal wealth manager/tax advisor to focus on *your* individual financial goals, while the accountant works closely with your CFO to manage the business's overall finances.

ROLE #2: M&A LAWYER

A top-notch mergers and acquisitions (M&A) lawyer differs from the personal lawyer who deals with your family matters. This is someone who specializes in transactions, specifically the sale of a business.

Look for a lawyer whose practice focuses 100% on representing buyers and sellers of companies, because they know the tricks that potential buyers use. Generalists might charge cheaper fees, but specialists are worth their weight in gold because they have the specific expertise and knowledge to negotiate the deal's terms. Remember: It's easy to get tunnel vision when talking prices, but *terms* often determine your post-transaction satisfaction and future liabilities. Don't get stuck in a situation where you've sold your business, only to end up bombarded by warranties, indemnities and liabilities that an M&A lawyer could have written off for you.

Consider term factors such as asset versus stock deals and seek the guidance of both your tax advisor and your M&A attorney to understand each option's implications and benefits. Your tax advisor might focus on the money you'll get from the sale and the taxes you'll need to pay, while your lawyer will have valuable opinions on what's holistically better for you as an entrepreneur. This opinion may be based on the type of business you're selling, the length of time you've been operational and your business history.

Don't think that you have to go with a blue chip or a prestigious NYC law or tax firm. Especially if your deal size is under $50 million, go with a smaller, local firm. You're less likely to get a first-year associate or intern, and more likely to receive deep expertise and attention from their most experienced people.

ROLE #3: INVESTMENT BANKER/BROKER/TRANSACTION ADVISER

Not every sale to private equity requires an investment banker, but this role can be critical in marketing your business and facilitating the transaction. You especially need an investment banker when you're about to go to market, although I personally don't think that transactions under $100M always need this representation.

When I'm involved early as an exit strategist, we may explore growth strategies and partnerships that can lead to a natural acquisition. This eliminates the need for an investment banker. But for most businesses, an experienced investment banker is an invaluable intermediary between you and a potential buyer. They manage your business sale and marketing materials, negotiations and the overall deal process. And when they have extensive experience in the field — they know what transactions in your market have or have not successfully closed — and they know the main buyers, they can significantly improve your transaction's outcome.

When choosing an investment banking firm, focus on finding the best fit for your specific needs. You don't want someone who will put you out to rot in a database somewhere. You want an engaged team that can deliver. Look for firms that understand your market and valuations, have successfully sold businesses in the past, and have the right expertise to handle your deal.

Are investment bankers expensive? They can be. But remember: This is the largest financial transaction of your life. The fees you'll pay are small relative to the outcome you aim to achieve.

Building the right advisory team is a critical aspect of Scale to Sale™. Experience has taught me that once you have the right team in place, everything else moves more efficiently. Having a personal tax advisor, wealth manager or financial advisor, specialized M&A lawyer, and experienced investment banker or transaction advisor empowers you to navigate a complex sale process with confidence. Don't cut corners. Invest in the right advisors to maximize your business' value and achieve the high-value exit you deserve. Understand what someone with experience (like me) actually brings to the table — effectively building, overseeing, quarterbacking this team.

Now that you know how to surround yourself with the best people and firms, it's time for the fifth and final step on the Scale to Sale™ process: your actual exit.

STEP 5: EXIT FOR THE HIGHEST MULTIPLE

Someone knocks on their door and says, "I want to buy your business." They reply, "Why, thank you very much!" And their business is magically sold. In reality, the owners who sell for the highest multiples make sure that the sale terms work in their favour. They engineer the entire exit process, and that's what this step is about.

I can tell you from my years on the private equity side of the table that PE orchestrates exits from the get-go. They know what's happening in the market, who's buying, who's selling, and where they're going to sell the business in the future. This final step of the Scale To Sale™ Methodology makes sure that *you* consider all of these factors before they do, so you can exit your business on *your own* terms and for the multiple that delivers *your life-changing number*.

Brace yourself. This section is a bit of a heavyweight. But I'll do my best to keep things concise.

First, remember that the process of selling your business for the highest multiple is both a science and an art. The science part is what we've discussed in the previous steps: creating predictability and dramatically increasing your chances of achieving a favourable outcome by the end of it. The art is navigating the world of buyers.

Is selling to PE largely a numbers game built on logic? Yes. But you also need to manage the *emotions* that come into play throughout the sales process, and those get trickier in the final stretch. It's like reaching the last mile of a marathon — and I know, I've run 67 of them! Once you see that finish line, everything you've been working so hard for becomes *real*, and your emotions can get the better of you.

Why is it so challenging? Because when you enter the universe of potential buyers, you encounter some true predators. These seasoned professionals buy out companies all the time, and they can easily sniff out a seller who doesn't know what they're doing.

I'm always amused when these guys realise that a business owner on the other side of the table has a capable and experienced team supporting them. Their heads go down. They sigh. They know they're going to have to take negotiations more seriously now, and the entire process is going to be more rigorous than they had hoped. "Oh no," they're thinking, "We're actually going to have to *work* for this!"

And this works in *your favour*, because now they're even more convinced of your company's value.

To put it bluntly: Come cautious. Returning to our house analogy, the world is filled with shady "flippers" who see you as the prey and not the prize. They thrive on buying undervalued businesses, "renovating" them quickly and selling them for a hefty multiple. The bigger the delta between the buying and selling prices, the more a PE Shark looks like a superstar to their buddies back at Club Hammerhead.

That's not your goal. You want to sell your business for the highest multiple and secure maximum value for it. So do that and let the buyers bear the risk. That's what this chapter is about.

As a refresher, let's review the different exit options available to you before we return our focus to private equity. The first fork in the road is deciding whether you want to sell *externally* or *internally*.

INTERNAL EXIT OPTIONS

These typically suit smaller businesses, especially those generating revenue under $10 million who find it hard to sell externally on the capital markets or to strategic buyers. The truth is that any business doing over $1M of EBITDA enters the firing line of PE, certainly as a bolt-on acquisition. Under $1M EBITDA is where the internal exit options become more relevant or selling to an "acquisition entrepreneur" in a deal which may not be as favourable to the seller as it is usually structured with a large chunk of seller financing. These exit options are limited to transferring ownership within the family or existing company structure. They include:

SELLING WITHIN THE FAMILY

In this scenario, you pass on ownership and control to your children through a succession deal. It usually doesn't result in the high multiple we're looking for, but selling to your offspring generally allows for a smooth transition.

Selling to Shareholders

Here, you sell to a current partner or shareholder within the business. If you have a 50/50 partnership, and you want to exit while your partner wants to continue running the business, you can sell some or all of your shares to your partner and maintain business continuity.

Selling to Management

If your business has capable managers who aren't yet shareholders, then a management buyout or management buy-in[71] may be suitable. These options involve the management team forming an entity to purchase your shares as the current owner. The potential for a high multiple is low, but you'll likely experience a straightforward transition since the managers are already familiar with your business.

Employee Share Ownership Scheme (ESOP)[72]

An ESOP, or *employee share ownership scheme*, is an intriguing exit option that grants employees the opportunity to acquire your business from you. It's popular among doctors and other professionals who want to pass their practice down. It can also provide tax advantages, especially in the U.K.

If you have a strong accountant or tax advisor on your deal team, they can go through the risks and opportunities attached to each of these internal exit options. But the best ones know that you're better off looking at *external selling options*. So, let's talk about those.

EXTERNAL EXIT OPTIONS

External exit options are better suited to larger businesses because they open up opportunities for strategic partnerships or financial transactions — both of which can lead to higher multiples and expanded growth prospects.

SELLING TO A FINANCIAL BUYER

Financial buyers acquire businesses so they can drive growth and maximize their investment. As you've learned, they ideally want to buy multiple assets, roll them up together and sell them as a group. If you sell to a financial buyer, you could be their *platform* acquisition (the first company they acquire in your industry before they buy others and bolt them onto you). Or you could be a *bolt-on* acquisition (added to their existing platform company within your market, sector or geography).

In either case, know the role a financial buyer expects you to play. They may already have their own leadership and management team in place, so they may not require your continued presence.

SELLING TO A STRATEGIC BUYER

Strategic buyers are usually larger corporations, public companies or entities backed by private equity (a.k.a. "PE-backed strategic"). Selling to a PE-backed strategic is like selling to a financial buyer in that your continued presence may or may not be needed after the ownership transfer. The PE firm backing your strategic buyer is essentially acquiring you as a bolt-on acquisition, so the strategic buyer is actually the platform company.

On the other hand, selling to a larger strategic buyer, or what I call a *corporate buyer*, can take on many different looks. These buyers may have different reasons for wanting to buy your business, so it won't be as linear or focused as selling to someone within the PE model. For example:

- If they're on the losing end of the war on talent, they might buy your business to access your talent pool.
- They might buy your business because you're advantageous to their growth plans (e.g., you have a product they'd love to sell to their customer base, and acquiring you allows them to expand their product line while avoiding R&D costs).
- They might want to buy your business because you're taking market share away from them now or might in the near future. As the saying goes, "It's better to kill the monster

while it's small." Facebook's early acquisition of Instagram is a good example of this.

- Some strategic buyers may also be pursuing their own exit strategy, such as an initial public offering (IPO). Acquiring your business adds your revenue and profit to theirs, boosts their attractiveness to investors and makes their eventual exit smoother and more profitable.

Understanding a strategic buyer's motivations and how your business aligns with their objectives helps in negotiations and in valuing your business. Many owners fail to appreciate that if someone buys their business for 5x EBITDA, and the entity buying is valued at 10x EBITDA, then the EBITDA they bring in from you is automatically valued at *theirs*.

In other words:

IF

A buyer wants to purchase you for 5 x $10 million, or $50 million.

AND

They're valued at 10x EBITDA.

THEN

That $50 million will be worth *$100 million* on their balance sheet.

"Hold on, let's make that $75 million," is what you say in this situation. Seriously, knowing this small detail could make you $25 million richer. A good exit advisor or investment banker should gain an understanding of the potential buyer's value and exit plan to improve your negotiating position.

LAUNCHING AN INITIAL PUBLIC OFFERING (IPO)

Rather than selling to a strategic buyer who's looking to launch an IPO, you could launch your own. But keep in mind that an IPO is more of a capital-raising event than a full exit. They also require specialized expertise and are most suited toward larger businesses with a significant market presence.

IPOs can also be expensive to construct (acquiring certain licenses, etc.). And even when they're successful, you're subject to new government regulations and rules for operations. There is also a delay in receiving pay-outs from sale of shares you do not have with other external sales where you have large sums deposited on the day of closing a deal.

When you IPO, any shares you sell as part of the public offering can be "held back" for a period of time to ensure the transition from private to public goes smoothly. I've seen as much as six months. So, in many cases, when you sell, you don't realize liquidity right away. Whereas when you sell to PE (or another strategic buyer), whatever is agreed as "cash at close" hits your bank account the day the Sale & Purchase Agreement is signed. So basically, immediate liquidity and in my opinion a cleaner transaction.

It's not uncommon for a newer business owner to be unaware of the complexities that accompany going public, or to hurt their business in the process. Many founders have taken their companies public, only to end up getting fired by the new board of directors. This is just one reason why I generally don't recommend IPOs as a first exit.

DOING A RECAPITALIZATION

This is basically refinancing your business and taking some cash off the table without selling it. You retain ownership while realising some of the value you've created. It can be an attractive option if you want to balance your desire for liquidity with staying involved in the business. Included here are *growth equity funds*[73].

LIQUIDATING YOUR BUSINESS

This involves winding down your business operations and taking out whatever value's left. It's not ideal, but if you haven't planned an exit strategy, can't find a viable internal or external sale option, fall ill, don't have a succession plan or can't find an interested buyer, it's a viable last resort.

Hopefully you now know why selling to a third-party strategic or financial buyer is the best way to achieve your high-value exit, and you have a strong idea of which specific option you would choose.

Financial vs. Strategic Buyers

Before we discuss the actual sales process and how you coordinate and exit for the highest multiple, let's dive deeper into the world of financial and strategic buyers. This is where the real game begins.

Strategic Buyers

When dealing with this kind of buyer, brace yourself. These guys often throw down the highest prices on the negotiation table. Why? Because it's all about synergies. When a strategic buyer swoops in, they bring their existing infrastructure, leadership teams and processes to the table. By integrating your assets into their setup, they can reduce costs and unleash a storm of value for themselves.

Strategic buyers thrive on acquisitions because they understand the power of buying and integrating businesses. But here's the catch: If you have dreams of sticking around and shaping the future of the business you built, a strategic buyer might not be your best bet. If they don't tell you that your services are no longer needed after the integration period (6–12 months), they'll often transform you into an *employee* and leave you yearning for the freedom and control you once enjoyed.

That said, if you're up-front about not wanting to stick around after the sale, then a strategic buyer might be just what you need. They can also play a unique role in the exit game because their mere presence can spark fierce battles among financial buyers. Competition is the name of the game here, and you can transform strategic buyers into powerful negotiating chips.

FINANCIAL BUYERS

Financial buyers are the titans of the private equity world. With a whopping *$4 trillion plus* in assets under management waiting to be deployed, they sit on mountains of cash (see Part Two: The Secret World of Private Equity). Typically, private equity firms and family offices[74], these financial buyers raise capital from eager investors who are even more eager for returns, and these firms need to deploy that money. If they don't, the investors get restless, and pressure mounts on the principals. Technically it's private equity firms that raise capital. The family offices already have access to capital from HNW and UHNW families[75], hence the distinction.

But here's what *really* sets financial buyers apart: They typically want you to stick around after the sale — especially if your business becomes their platform. Remember, financial buyers aren't business owners or entrepreneurs by nature. They're financial wizards who excel at creating value on profit-and-loss statements and balance sheets. To turn their investment into a success story, they need your leadership and management prowess.

If you're *not* their platform acquisition, but rather one of their coveted bolt-ons, then financial buyers may have different plans for you. They might not require your presence after the sale, or they might want you to join the leadership team they've already assembled. If you dream of selling your business multiple times and being part of a grand roll-up strategy, then joining forces with a financial buyer is the way to go.

But wait, there's more. With financial buyers, you have the incredible opportunity to roll over some of the money from your initial exit into the new entity. Picture this: selling your business not just once, but twice or more, and reaping the rewards *multiple times over.* That's the kind of power financial buyers bring to the table, and this concept of significant wealth creation didn't exist before private equity.

PRICING & VALUE

As we wade further into *your* exit journey, remember: Time can kill all deals, and this is a key difference between strategic and financial buyers. Because they're often big corporations, strategic buyers are known for moving at a glacial pace. In the fast-paced world of exits, slow can equal death. So, while strategic buyers have their merits, their sluggishness might not align with your desired timeline.

Here's another golden nugget of advice:

> If you're interested in the strategic play, consider forming partnerships with potential strategic acquirers long before you're ready to exit.

By engaging in commercial joint ventures and establishing mutually beneficial relationships, you can build trust while you gauge how they operate. Many successful high-value acquisitions are born from these strategic partnerships. It's a low-risk way to pave your exit path and potentially accelerate your timing. Partnerships can also accelerate your business growth at the same time.

There's no one-size-fits-all solution for exiting your business. The decision ultimately lies in *your* hands and will be shaped by *your* ambitions, goals and aspirations. Do you yearn to stay at the helm and drive the growth of the entity you've built, or do you want a massive payday that will fling open the doors to life's next exciting journey?

Whichever path you choose, be prepared for the high-stakes game that lies ahead. Embrace the dance between financial and strategic buyers. Leverage the competition. Come to the negotiating table over-prepared. Navigate with certainty and finesse. And be the prize, not the prey.

This is the pinnacle of your entrepreneurial journey, where you can unlock unimaginable rewards and make your mark on the business world.

Next, let's unravel the secrets of coordinating your exit *for the highest multiple* regardless of whether you choose to sell to a strategic or financial buyer. Thanks to their deep pockets, strategic buyers can indeed drive up the price of your business. But don't discount the competitive landscape of financial buyers.

When multiple PE firms set their sights on your business, they'll wage a fierce battle to win your favour. You hold the cards. If you've diligently followed the advice of building value, their offers may soar higher than they initially intended and leave you with a smile on your face and some additional life-changing cash in your pocket.

Selling Stock vs. Assets

You generally sell a business in the form of an asset sale or a stock sale. In an **asset sale**, someone buys your business and strips the assets in whole or part (for example, a buyer might be after your IP or customer base, but not other assets). In a **stock sale** or **shares sale**, someone buys your entire business.

I sometimes think of the analogy of buying a cow: An *asset sale* is buying the cow to eat the steak. You kill the cow and get a one-off benefit. Whereas a *stock sale* is buying the cow for the milk. You want the cow fit and healthy to keep producing milk now and into the future. Both are valuable. One is short term; the other is more sustainable.

THE END-TO-END SALE PROCESS

We've walked the first four steps of the Scale To Sale™ Methodology. You know the different exit options. And you understand why a strategic or financial buyer will most likely be the one to deliver your life-changing financial number. Let's bring it home by walking through the end-to-end sales process.

This is another multi-part process, but don't be intimidated. We've already touched on many of these steps in previous chapters. Now I'm going to bring them together so we can craft your most lucrative business exit.

STEP #1: COMPLETE YOUR DEAL TEAM

We've talked about the deal team you've already started building as part of Step 4. If you've assembled a formidable group that includes your value or exit advisor, lawyer, tax accountant and financial capability experts, then you've already laid the groundwork for a successful exit.

Depending on whether you've found a buyer through a partnership or are looking to take your business to market in some form of auction process, now would be a good time to complete the roster and add an investment banker and/or corporate finance specialist. Strike the right balance between internal and external specialists, and make sure everyone is laser-focused on executing a successful transaction.

The size of your business often determines the size of your deal team. At the very least, you'll need financial and legal representation. However, don't underestimate the impact of your internal team, particularly your C-suite or leadership team. Your Chief Operating Officer (COO), and Chief Financial Officer (CFO) might be involved in due diligence, management presentations and various other critical tasks.

Pro Tip

Don't run your business and exit process at the same time. If you have a capable second-in-command, divide and conquer. Have your team run the business for the next 6–9 months while you explore the external part of the process. Start working with your investment banker and get more involved in your exit options and looking for acquirers. This will ensure that the exit process runs well while the business continues to grow.

Don't let your business suffer. It's easy to lose sight of day-to-day operations. A lengthy sales process can span nine to twelve months, which poses a risk to your business's performance that astute PE firms might exploit as a negotiation point called a *retrade,* when the amount offered in the LOI (Letter of Intent) is more than the final offer. This often happens when the business performance has declined throughout the due diligence (DD) and sales process due to management getting distracted. Stay vigilant and ensure that your leadership team keeps a firm grip on the business's reins.

Having a well-rounded deal team in place is an absolute game-changer. It's critical early on, and it grows even more important as you enter the sales process. These experts guide you through the intricacies of negotiations, due diligence and valuation while protecting your interests and maximizing the value of your business.

STEP #2: COMPLETE YOUR STRATEGIC POSITIONING & PREPARATION

With your *dream deal team* in place, it's time to dive deeper into uncovering the true value of your business and how you effectively communicate it to potential buyers.

First, visibility. Mark your territory and catch the attention of potential acquirers early on. Even financial buyers should be on your radar. Identify private equity firms specializing in your industry or sector and get to know them by attending industry events, speaking engagements or even private equity conferences. Don't go with the sole intention of selling your business. Focus on raising awareness and doing your own research on the market instead. As you learn about valuations in the industry and deals that have recently taken place, these connections can be invaluable.

A burning question I often encounter is whether to opt for a broad sales auction process or a more targeted approach. That depends on your ideal outcome and future plans. I strongly advise that you target partnerships early on as part of your growth strategy. If the partners turn into potential acquirers, these partnerships will add value while mitigating complexity and cost.

If you prefer a more discreet approach than a broad auction process, then a closed auction might be the way to go. This involves positioning your business strategically, identifying potential buyers, and understanding their needs and preferences. This is where that investment banker or corporate finance specialist plays a crucial role. They bridge their market knowledge with your advisory team's expertise to position your business for a successful sale.

This is also the time to conduct buyer due diligence. Get to know your industry's key players who are actively acquiring businesses. Which events do they attend? What recent acquisitions have they made? Take a closer look at their culture and integration practices. Can you envision yourself being part of their future growth?

The same goes for financial buyers. Is the PE firm a good fit for your aspirations? Do they understand and appreciate the value of working collaboratively with business owners? This research will help you align your positioning and prepare for fruitful conversations with potential acquirers.

Your Exit Story

Your exit story is the *beginning* of your pitch — not the pitch you'll ultimately use in your presentation, but the story of why your business is valuable and perfectly positioned to transition to a new owner. It's a growth story. It's not about what you want, but what your business is primed to do in the future. The more you can paint a picture of making acquisitions and winning big customers, the more attractive you'll be before going to market, and the better able you'll be to flex that multiple.

STEP #3: CONSIDER VALUATION, TERMS & TIMING

We've talked about how private equity and strategic buyers traditionally assess value by looking at the last three years of net profit (EBITDA) and applying a multiple, but more recently these sophisticated buyers look at the *trailing 12 months* (TTM)[76] performance. Why? Because the world moves more quickly, and a realistic value determination looks at a company's *run rate*[77] versus its historical performance — especially over a focused time period.

To sell on your terms, consider the forecast year as well. This is your company's projected performance over the *next* 12 months. The last three years and trailing year provide an actual number, but that number may not capture your company's increasing growth potential. Including the *projected* EBITDA of the forecast year in your valuation can boost the final price.

Beyond the valuation amount, understand the *terms* of the deal. When you receive an offer, it usually comes in the form of a non-binding agreement called a *letter of intent* (LOI). Based on a preliminary assessment of your financials, this agreement triggers a period of exclusivity during which the buyer conducts due diligence.

Deal terms cover the transaction's structure and how you'll be paid. Typically, you won't receive the full payment upfront. Instead, you'll receive a portion (usually 50%–70%) upon closing the deal. The remaining amount may be structured as an *earnout*[78], where you receive payments based on the business's performance over a specified period. Remember there are time-based earn-outs as well as performance-based earn-outs. Time-based is about how long you stay after the transaction has been completed If the buyer is financial, it can also be rolled over into the new entity created by the buyer.

Understanding deal terms also involves considering factors like working capital. Buyers expect the business to have sufficient working capital to operate smoothly after the sale.

Cash-Free, Debt-Free

All businesses are sold on a cash-free, debt-free basis. That means any cash in the business can be taken out by the seller, minus whatever is agreed as working capital. Equally, any debt in the business comes off the final valuation (e.g., a business worth $50 million with $8 million in debt will be valued at $42 million).

The negotiation of working capital can significantly impact the amount of cash you receive at closing. Additionally, the terms encompass other aspects like warranties, indemnities and any risks associated with the business.

Timing is another important consideration. You may want to sell your business at the peak of the market, but it's more effective to assess whether the market conditions are generally strong (with high multiples in your industry), then align your exit strategy accordingly. Rest assured, exceptional businesses with unique qualities and transferable value can still achieve significant sales and high multiples in less favourable market conditions.

Businesses that are well-constructed and exit-ready will always sell for high multiples, regardless of market conditions.

STEP #4: TAKE YOUR BUSINESS TO MARKET

Once your business is primed for the highest valuation, it's time to engage your investment banker or corporate finance specialist to let potential buyers know that your business is for sale.

This phase begins with a *teaser* document, a brief overview of your business and market designed to generate interest from potential buyers without revealing specific company details. Simultaneously, you and your team must prepare an *information memorandum* that provides in-depth information about your business. When you hire an investment banker, marketing materials are part of what you pay for. So, they'll usually produce this document, as well as assist with management presentation materials.

As expressions of interest come in, your investment banker will assist in assessing the non-binding letters of intent (LOIs), helping you compare multiple offers to evaluate their prices and terms.

After selecting a few potential buyers, they'll conduct preliminary due diligence. A more detailed information memorandum will be shared, and management presentations will be conducted. This stage allows buyers to delve deeper into your business through a *data room*[79] and gather more information for their formal offers.

Eventually, you'll choose the buyer with the best offer, mix of price and terms, and enter into exclusivity, indicating your preferred deal partner. Once exclusivity is established, a thorough due diligence process begins, typically lasting around 60-90 days. This stage involves more in-depth investigations into your business's operations and financials — a critical step before doing final negotiations and closing the deal.

The entire marketing and negotiation process can span several weeks or months and requires careful considerations of offers, terms and compatibility with your objectives. With the guidance of your investment banker and exit advisor, you'll navigate this journey and work toward a successful sale.

STEP #5: ENTERTAIN, NEGOTIATE, MITIGATE

After due diligence, you'll receive the final offer for your business. In this critical moment, your company's value can rise, or fall based on how well you've built it and how well you've managed business performance during the sales process. If you've followed the strategies outlined in this book and created an exceptional business, the offer may *increase*. On the other hand, financial buyers can act like homebuyers looking for bad windows or siding to justify an offer *decrease*.

Beware of *re-trading*

"A re-trade occurs when the potential buyer of a company reduces the amount of their original offer... and it will cost the seller heavily to back out of the transaction. ... A re-trade can be seen as a form of power play on the part of the buyer... Re-trades can also happen for legitimate reasons ... During the due diligence process, the buyer may discover a flaw or shortcoming in the business being sold and thus lower its bid accordingly."

—https://www.divestopedia.com/definition/6745/re-trade/

If you continue to show growth during the selling process (e.g., acquiring a large client, showing greater profits than expected), you can affect a re-trade that *increases* your final price. You will need to lead this part of the negotiation, but if in fact there is a legitimate case for an increase because the business is growing rapidly, this can be a power play in its own right. It can force a prospective buyer to close more quickly to mitigate an increasing valuation.

To mitigate potential issues before entering the final stages of the exit process, conduct your own shadow due diligence.

During negotiations, pay close attention to the transaction's structure — including pricing, terms and potential concessions made in the late stages. Review warranties and indemnities with the help of a skilled M&A lawyer. Avoid ongoing risks or liabilities that may arise post-sale. Additionally, consider obtaining insurance coverage for certain risks, even though it can be costly.

Time periods also play a significant role in negotiations. The length of an earn-out agreement that requires you to stay involved in the business depends on your goals and circumstances. Understanding and addressing these elements will ensure that you're well-prepared for the concluding phase of the sale process.

STEP #6: CRAFT THE DEFINITIVE AGREEMENTS

The final phase of your exit process involves drafting and finalizing the agreements that will govern the entire transaction. *The most crucial document in this stage is the sale and purchase agreement* (SPA). Engage your M&A lawyer to thoroughly review this complex document. Pay close attention to any ancillary fees or payments that may need to be returned if certain conditions aren't met. As discussed during negotiations, the SPA should address price adjustments, non-compete clauses, restrictions on staff retention and other relevant terms.

If your business includes real estate, determine how it'll be treated in the transaction. Will the new owner lease or purchase the property? If you've agreed to remain with the company for a specified period, you'll need to negotiate an employment agreement. Clarify whether you'll be employed as the CEO or consultant, and discuss salary, bonuses and any additional compensation separate from the deal.

Some final reminders:

- As I've emphasized throughout this book, remember the significance of having the right team by your side. A perfect exit requires a well-prepared end-game assessment, understanding the value you want to sell for, and assembling the ideal internal leadership and advisory teams.

- Maintain sell-side control: Lead the process rather than letting the buyers dictate it. Time your sale strategically and conduct shadow due diligence to anticipate how the potential buyer's due diligence will unfold. If necessary, orchestrate buyer competition to maximize your options.

- Unless you're enticed by the idea of rolling over funds into the new entity, secure as much cash at closing as possible. Strive for an amount that aligns with your life-changing number. Future payments may not materialize once you lose control of the business. Minimize earnouts and deferred payments, focusing more on time-based earnouts rather than performance-based ones. Above all, put proper tax mitigation strategies in place to eliminate, minimize or defer taxes.

- Separate your deal team from your business operations. *Private equity firms may slow down a deal when a business is struggling so they can acquire it at a lower valuation.* Conversely, if your business is thriving and experiencing rapid growth, PE will try to expedite the transaction to pay a higher price. Incubate these two areas to position yourself in the best possible way.

- Set the elements for this process well in advance of your intended exit so you can sell your business for the highest multiple, on *your* terms, without getting undermined by sophisticated buyers.

INTEGRATION

Congratulations, you've sold your business!

Once your sale and purchase agreement is signed, you've exited your company. And if you've followed the insights in this book, you've done so for the highest multiple and on terms that will help you move on to your next chapter.

However, many business owners make a big mistake at this point: Even though integration is discussed all the way through the end-to-end sales process, they spend too little time on *post-sale integration.* At this point in the process, they realize that they've lost all control.

If your earnout will be based on numbers you set in advance for future performance, set realistic expectations. If you want key management team members and others to stick around, make sure you've incentivized them to do so. Specifically, make sure you have some say in what a sophisticated buyer negotiates for their new employment terms. Also do some work to ensure that your company culture fits with the culture of the buyer's business.

A deal can go backwards if it's made purely on the numbers. Protect yourself against this by agreeing on a timeline for integration — say, 12 months — so certain aspects of your business can be slowly incorporated into the new company.

The more you prepare for integration in advance, the more enjoyable the process will be, the lower the chances your business will go backwards after the sale, and you will lose your earn-out.

ORCHESTRATING THE PERFECT EXIT

Successful Exit Characteristics

01 FINANCIAL PERFORMANCE

Specific focus on:

- Quality of earnings
- Revenue Growth
- Margin expansion
- Strong EBITDA position within category
- Strong balance sheet for debt leverage

02 GROWTH STRATEGY

Clear understanding and application of:

- Organic growth - marketing + sales
- Strategic growth - partnerships, JVs, M&A
- Opportunities + risks

03 BUSINESS MODEL

"Simplicity scales ... Complexity fails"

Simple business model that is:

- Predictable
- Repeatable
- Sustainable
- Transferable (Intangible assets)

04 MARKET POSITIONING (STORY)

What market are we really in?

- Certain markets are more valuable at certain times ... with defined characteristics and value drivers

Exit strategy/planning should start 12 to 36 months before a sales process starts!

The Perfect Exit?

- ✓ Clear understanding of enterprise value - financial vs. strategic
- ✓ Partnerships created for scale (and possible exit)
- ✓ Assembling the perfect "deal" team - internal + external
- ✓ Sell-side control (timing and value, thorough due diligence in advance)
- ✓ Orchestrating buyer competition (if required)
- ✓ Cash maximization at close
- ✓ Minimal earn out or deferred payments (time vs. performance based)
- ✓ Tax mitigation - eliminating, minimizing or deferring - well in advance

KEY TAKEAWAYS

- SCALE TO SALE™ is the proprietary methodology I use as a framework for scaling a company to a high-value exit. This is where we apply the principles of private equity to your business. The five Scale To Sale™ steps are:

  1. Establish a Clear End Game
  2. Strengthen Your Foundations
  3. Growth: Scale Fast & Expand Value
  4. Prepare & Profit Up
  5. Exit for the Highest Multiple.

- Build an advisory team that includes a personal tax advisor/wealth advisor, M&A lawyer and investment banker/broker/transaction adviser, and of course, an exit/value advisor.
- Determine your "life-changing number": the sale price for your business that will truly change your life and create financial independence. Determine why it matters and how far away from it you currently are.
- Don't just put a valuation on your future business; imagine what it will actually look and feel like.
- Figure out *early* the role you want to play in your business after you sell it. Do you still want to be involved in some way, or are you ready to completely hand over the reins?
- You can sell your company internally (to a partner, employees or management team) or externally (strategic or financial buyer). You can also launch an IPO, but that's more of a capital-raising tool than a true exit.

- "Multiples" are the name of the game. Your industry has a standard EBITDA multiple range. Your goal is to get your business to the point where it's worth the high end of that range.
- Only 30%–40% of your company's value comes from its financials. The other 60%–70% comes from intangibles: your people, processes, proposition (reputation/culture), protection (legal/compliance) and profitability.
- Map your Talent to Value: Look across your *entire* organization to identify the roles that create the most value, then place the right talent in those places.
- You can grow your business through organic growth (adding customers, increasing prices and/or sales) and strategic growth (leveraging networks, partnerships/joint ventures, mergers and acquisitions, and accessing and structuring capital).
- Most business owners focus purely on organic growth, but strategic growth is critical.
- Preparing and profiting up is like the stage of selling a house where you take down the scaffolding, clean up and stage your home to look perfect to a potential buyer. A key element of this is preparing your own Quality of Earnings report.
- Your overall goal is to create a "transferrable asset." That means your business can't depend too much on *you*, which is a hard emotional step for many business owners to take.
- Your compelling growth/exit story showcases your company's value to buyers who are betting on its future success. It goes beyond highlighting past achievements to focus on the growth trajectory that makes your business an attractive investment opportunity.
- If you're interested in going with a strategic buyer, consider forming partnerships with various strategic players long before you're ready to exit. By engaging in commercial joint ventures

and establishing mutually beneficial relationships, you can build trust while gauging how these entities operate and grow your business at the same time.

- After you successfully sell your business, don't forget about *post-sale integration.* If your earnout will be based on numbers you set in advance for future performance, set realistic expectations. If you want key management team members to stick around, incentivize them to do so.

EPILOGUE:

YOUR NEXT CHAPTER: PRIZE OR PREY?

I COULD HAVE started *Exit for Millions* with this chapter. Not because it's more important than everything that came before—but because without understanding this piece, the rest of it can fall apart. I've seen it too many times: a founder spends 20, sometimes 30 years building a company. They pour everything into it—sleepless nights, years of sacrifice, all in service of that one big goal… the exit. They dream of that moment for so long it starts to take on mythic weight. It becomes the purpose behind every decision, the payoff for every hard season. They imagine the day it happens—how it'll feel to see the wire hit the account, to finally breathe, to toast the people who mattered most on the journey.

And yet, when that day comes, too often it lands with a thud.

The reality isn't champagne and a packed-out celebration. It's *silence*. It's *stillness*. It's a quiet dinner with a partner or a small circle of family, often too exhausted from the process to feel joy. It's waking up the next morning and wondering: *Now what?* Because when the singular goal you've worked toward for decades is suddenly achieved, the space it leaves behind can feel... empty. Like you're holding a map with no destination.

And that's what I want to talk about now. While this book is about creating a high-value business and engineering a life-changing exit, it's about more than those, it's about identity, purpose, and designing what happens after the deal is done.

When I say prize or prey, I'm not just talking about how buyers perceive your business. I'm talking about how you perceive yourself when the business is no longer yours. If your identity has been wrapped up in "Founder" or "CEO" for 10, 20, 30 years... who are you when that's no longer true? When the staff no longer looks to you? When your calendar is suddenly wide open, and there are no urgent fires to put out?

Some founders feel a deep sense of liberation in that. Others, quietly, feel lost. Some even experience what I call exit depression—a kind of emotional whiplash that comes from reaching the mountain peak and realizing you never planned for the descent. This isn't uncommon. In fact, it's so common I now encourage every client to think about what's next before they even begin the exit process. And that's why I'm ending the book with this—not as a warning, but as an invitation.

The real game doesn't end at the exit, it starts after it. And now you've got the playbook. You understand what creates *enterprise value*. You know how to scale without chaos, how to lead without burning out, how to build a business that buyers don't just notice but chase. You've learned the principles of private equity, the power of the five growth levers, and how to apply the Scale to Sale™ Methodology to unlock a truly life-changing outcome.

And now it's time to get honest about something deeper: What's the vision beyond the exit? What kind of life are you stepping into? Because goals aren't just destinations. They're identities we step into. As I said earlier in the book, a goal isn't something you move toward—it's something you come from. If you don't create a compelling vision for what comes after the business, you risk drifting. And drift leads to doubt, regret, or worst of all—sabotage.

This is why so many founders get cold feet before signing the deal. It's not the valuation. It's not the tax consequences. It's the lack of a *why* that pulls them forward into their next chapter. So, let's ask the hard questions:

Why do you really want to sell?

What are you moving toward, not just away from?

What will your days look like when you no longer have to do anything?

What's your purpose when financial independence is no longer a goal, but a given?

And what will truly light you up?

For some, it's philanthropy. A foundation. Giving back. For others, it's finally writing that book, traveling with their partner, spending time with their kids before they leave home, or learning how to enjoy stillness for the first time in years.

For others still, it's building again—but smarter this time. Buying companies instead of starting them. Becoming an acquirer. An investor. Someone who builds generational wealth through strategy, not hustle. That's the power of a high-value exit. You buy back your time, your energy, your freedom—and your options. And options, my friend, are the ultimate luxury.

This is why I push founders to create a Vivid Vision—not just for their company, but for their life. Your future deserves the same clarity and structure you gave your business. Write it down. Build a vision board. Picture your next ten years with detail and colour. Will you live part-time in another country? Mentor other entrepreneurs? Build a family office? Or simply unplug, rest, and reconnect with yourself?

None of these answers are wrong. The only mistake is not choosing one. Because if you don't decide who you want to become after the exit, someone—or something—else will decide for you. And if you're like many of the founders I work with, you won't stop at just one exit. Once you've done it once—once you've experienced the process, seen how the game is played from the inside—you'll realise you can do it again. Smarter. Faster. With less stress and more leverage.

Maybe you'll build a portfolio of businesses. Maybe you'll become a growth-stage investor. Maybe you'll engineer two or three exits a year instead of working on one for the next 20. This is what the best in private equity do. They play the long game with repeatable moves. And it's how they build wealth that lasts generations.

You can do the same.

Let me leave you with this: Years ago, I was the one they called when things needed to change—fast. I sat at the boardroom table, ran the companies, closed the deals. Private equity trained me to see value where others missed it, to scale with precision, and to exit with impact. But over time, something changed. I stopped doing it for investors.

And I started doing it for founders. I saw too many great entrepreneurs lose the game—not because they didn't work hard, but because they never learned how the game was actually played.

I wrote this book so you wouldn't be one of them. Not just to show you how to build a business that's worth millions, but to show you how to build a life that's worth living on your terms. A life of freedom. Of purpose. Of options. The boardroom taught me how to create enterprise value. But it's this next chapter—this personal one—that teaches you how to turn that value into meaning.

You already know how to build. Now you know how to scale. And soon, when the time is right, you'll know how to exit.

What happens next is entirely up to you. But whatever you choose, make sure you choose it *powerfully*. Because the most valuable thing you'll ever own is not your business.

It's your story.

And you're just getting started.

About the Author

NICK BRADLEY is a globally recognised author, speaker, and business growth expert - known for helping founders scale fast, exit smart, and maximise the value of what they've built.

With over a decade of experience in private equity, Nick has led over 50 acquisitions and 27 successful exits - including three deals valued at more than $1 billion. His work has generated over $5 billion in enterprise value, giving him a deep understanding of how high-level investors and private equity firms assess, grow, and sell businesses for maximum return.

He is the creator of the Scale to Sale™ Methodology - a proven framework designed to help founders grow with precision and prepare their companies for high-value exits. His mission is to level the playing field by giving business owners the same strategies, tools, and insights used by top-tier investors and sophisticated acquirers.

Nick is also the host of Scale Up with Nick Bradley, a top-ranked business podcast with more than one million downloads across 130 countries. The show features global business leaders including Seth Godin, Patrick Bet-David, Amy Porterfield, Jay Abraham, and Neil Patel.

Nick believes successful exits aren't random - they're engineered.

He helps ambitious founders think like investors, act like CEOs, and exit on their terms.

Your Next Step

AS WE WRAP up perhaps our first journey together in this book, I think it's best to remind you that *most businesses don't sell for the value the business owner wants.* In fact, most businesses either don't sell at all (only 20% of businesses doing under $10 million in revenues sell), or they don't sell for the price or terms the business owner wants. But in your case, you've just learned first-hand how to be part of the successful minority who have created high-value exits for their themselves. In fact, you now possess knowledge that surpasses that of most business owners. You understand the inner workings of private equity. The insights you have gained from this book will *exponentially* enable you to do and achieve better than most, and you are now one of the enlightened few who really comprehend what potential buyers are seeking. You now fully grasp the concept of *transfer value*, realising that it extends beyond mere financial performance. Instead, it encompasses building a business with a solid foundation, capable of generating consistent financial success and propelling future growth. This transfer value is precisely what entices buyers to pay top dollar for your business.

So, in closing, I hope you now see how your future is in your own hands. You can exit with a bang or a whimper. I'm here to guide you wherever it is you truly want to go. It's exactly what I love doing and exactly why I switched sides of the negotiating table and live a fulfilling life. My highest hope is that I've convinced you to take the right steps towards the high-value exit you deserve after all these years of painstakingly working on your business.

So, what's your next step?

I often say be grateful, be brave, have faith, and show up. If you're ready to dive into this journey and want to capitalise on the potential of a high-value exit, I encourage you to visit my website:

I am delighted to offer you a complimentary consultation with one of our esteemed exit strategists. They will provide valuable insights and advice on the areas you should focus on to elevate your chances of achieving a high-value exit. It's a simple process, really. Just visit the website and book your free strategy call.

From there, we can chart the course toward your desired outcome together.

SCALE UP
WITH NICK BRADLEY

THE U.K.'S #1 BUSINESS PODCAST. With over *1 million* downloads in 130 countries, the show regularly attracts over 20,000 listeners per month.

In his podcast, Nick connects with the most remarkable people to show listeners how to scale up their business and their life. To achieve greater freedom, wealth, impact, and live life on their terms.

Guests include: Neil Patel / Daniel Priestley / Evan Carmichael / Tony Horton / Rob Moore / Oren Klaff / John Lee Dumas / Zach Bitter / Rock Thomas / Patrick Bett-David / James Altucher / Gino Wickman / Jay Abraham / Anthony Trucks / David Meltzer / Robin Sharma... and more.

GLOSSARY

assets under management (AUM): "Assets under management (AUM) is the market value of the investments managed by a person or entity on behalf of clients. AUM is used in conjunction with management performance and management experience when evaluating a company. When calculating AUM, some financial institutions include bank deposits, mutual funds, and cash, while others limit it to funds under discretionary management from individual investors" (https://www.investopedia.com/terms/a/aum.asp)

buy and build strategy: "… when a company expands its operations by acquiring a platform company with developed expertise that it can then build out. When a business requires growth and expansion… it can buy a business with an already developed expertise in that area of specialization and build it out further."

(https://corporatefinanceinstitute.com/resources/management/buy-and-build-strategy/)

C-suite: "… the upper echelons of a corporation's senior executives and managers. C-suite gets its name from the titles of top senior executives, which tend to start with the letter C, for "chief," as in chief executive officer (CEO), chief financial officer (CFO), chief operating officer (COO), and chief information officer (CIO)." (https://www.investopedia.com/terms/c/c-suite.asp)

capital call: "A capital call, also known as a 'draw down,' is the act of collecting funds from limited partners whenever the need arises. When an investor buys into a private equity fund, the firm makes an agreement with the investor that these funds will be available when the firm requests them. In turn, investors are able to hold onto their funds and keep them in a favorable investment account, such as a mutual fund or retirement account, so that the investment can continue to appreciate until the firm needs it." (https://www.securedocs.com/blog/private-equity-what-is-a-capital-call)

capital markets: "… are venues where savings and investments are channelled between suppliers and those in need of capital." (https://www.investopedia.com/terms/c/capitalmarkets.asp)

carried interest: "Carried interest, or 'carry' for short, is the percentage of a private fund's investment profits that a fund manager receives as compensation. Used primarily by private equity funds, including venture capital funds, carry is one of the primary ways fund managers are paid." (—https://carta.com/learn/private-funds/management/carried-interest/)

commoditized market: "A market is commoditized when competing products are effectively interchangeable and therefore customers make decisions based solely on price." (https://www.merriam-webster.com/dictionary/commoditized)

compound annual growth rate (CAGR): "The compound annual growth rate (CAGR) is the mean annual growth rate of an investment over a period longer than one year. It's one of the most accurate ways to calculate and determine returns for individual assets, investment portfolios, and anything that can rise or fall in value over time." (https://www.investopedia.com/investing/compound-annual-growth-rate-what-you-should-know/)

delta: "… a difference between two things or values." (Google definition)

distributed to paid-in capital (DPI): "… is a financial metric used in the context of private equity and venture capital investments. It measures the ratio of cash distributions that investors have received from a venture capital or private equity fund to the total capital they initially invested in the fund." (https://inc42.com/glossary/distributed-to-paid-in-capital/)

distribution: "Distributions, the means by which private equity funds return capital to investors, are paid when fund managers realise their investments in underlying companies or assets." (—https://www.moonfare.com/blog/private-equity-distributions)

earnout: An earnout is a contractual provision stating that the seller of a business is to obtain additional compensation in the future if the business achieves certain financial goals, which are usually stated as a percentage of gross sales or earnings. (https://www.investopedia.com/terms/e/earnout.asp)

EBITDA: "… earnings before interest, taxes, depreciation, and amortization, is a metric used to measure a company's financial health and ability to generate cash flow." (https://www.businessnewsdaily.com/4461-ebitda-formula-definition.html)

enterprise multiple: ... a ratio used to determine the value of a company ... Enterprise multiples can vary depending on the industry. Higher enterprise multiples are expected in high-growth industries and lower multiples in industries with slow growth. (https://www.investopedia.com/terms/e/ev-ebitda.asp)

exponential growth: Exponential growth is the compounding effect when combining organic and strategic growth strategies, the result being an increase in both scale and speed of growth. By combining organic and strategic growth strategies, you get there faster, and you get a bigger result.

financial buyer: "… long-term investors interested in the return that they can get by buying a well-managed company. Financial buyers look to generate cash flow by boosting revenue, cutting costs, or creating economies of scale by buying similar companies." (https://www.investopedia.com/terms/f/financial-buyer.asp)

fractional CFO: A fractional CFO is an experienced finance professional who provides services for organizations in a part-time, retainer, or contract arrangement. They offer a company the experience and expertise of a high-end CFO without the in-house cost of a full-time hire. (https://preferredcfo.com/what-is-fractional-cfo/)

fractional finance team: "… when companies need senior, strategic leadership in the finance function to partner with the CEO, but the role does not yet warrant a full-time position." (https://fractionalfinance.co/)

general partner (in private equity): "… general partners have full operational control of a business and unlimited liability, in the business sense. Limited partners have less liability and do not take part in day-to-day business operations." (https://www.shopify.com/blog/general-vs-limited-partnership)

horizontal expansion: "… also known as lateral or horizontal integration, involves merging two or more companies with similar operation or production processes in the supply chain. In essence, a company moves to perform more services or produce more goods on the same part of the supply chain." (https://study.com/academy/lesson/horizontal-expansion-in-business-definition-examples.html)

internal rate of return (IRR): "... the interest rate (also known as the discount rate) that will bring a series of cash flows (positive and negative) to a net present value (NPV) of zero or to the current value of cash invested. Investors and firms use IRR to evaluate whether an investment in a project can be justified." (https://www.investopedia.com/terms/i/internal-rate-of-return-rule.asp)

IPO: "IPO stands for initial public offering. As the name suggests, it signifies the first time a stock is made available to the public on an exchange—like the New York Stock Exchange (NYSE) or Nasdaq—to buy and sell." (https://www.schwab.com/learn/story/what-is-an-ipo)

joint venture (JV): A joint venture (JV) is a business arrangement in which two or more parties agree to pool their resources for the purpose of accomplishing a specific task. This task can be a new project or any other business activity. Each of the participants in a joint venture is responsible for profits, losses, and costs associated with it. However, the venture is its own entity, separate from the participants' other business interests. (https://www.investopedia.com/terms/j/jointventure.asp)

key performance indicator (KPI): "... a quantifiable measure of performance over time for a specific objective." (https://www.qlik.com/us/kpi)

lifetime value (LTV): "... the total revenue a company expects to earn over the lifetime of their relationship with a single customer." (https://corporatefinanceinstitute.com/resources/valuation/lifetime-value-calculation/)

limited partner (in private equity): "A Limited Partner (LP) in the context of private equity or venture capital, is an individual or an entity that contributes capital to a fund but does not participate in its management. These are often institutions like pension funds, insurance companies, foundations, or wealthy individuals." (https://www.bunch.capital/private-markets-glossary/lp-limited-partner-co-investor)

long tail: "… a business strategy that allows companies to realize significant profits by selling low volumes of hard-to-find items to many customers, instead of only selling large volumes of a reduced number of popular items." (https://www.investopedia.com/terms/l/long-tail.asp)

low-churn business model: "Churn rate, also known as attrition rate or customer churn, is the rate at which customers stop doing business with an entity." (https://www.investopedia.com/terms/c/churnrate.asp)

market capitalization ("cap"): "Market capitalization shows how much a company is worth as determined by the total market value of all outstanding shares. To calculate a company's market cap, multiply the number of outstanding shares by the current market value of one share." (https://www.investopedia.com/terms/m/marketcapitalization.asp)

mergers and acquisitions (M&A): A merger is an agreement that unites two existing companies into one new company. There are several types of mergers and reasons companies complete mergers. Mergers and acquisitions (M&A) are commonly done to expand a company's reach, expand into new segments, or gain market share. All of these are done to increase shareholder value. Often, during a merger, companies have a no-shop clause to prevent purchases or mergers by additional companies. (https://www.investopedia.com/terms/m/merger.asp)

minimum / required / preferred rate of return: "The required rate of return (hurdle rate) is the minimum return that an investor is expecting to receive for their investment. Essentially, the required rate is the minimum acceptable compensation for the investment's level of risk. The required rate of return is a key concept in corporate finance and equity valuation."

(https://corporatefinanceinstitute.com/resources/career-map/sell-side/capital-markets/required-rate-of-return/)

multiple: "Enterprise multiple... is a ratio used to determine the value of a company... Enterprise multiples can vary depending on the industry. Higher enterprise multiples are expected in high-growth industries and lower multiples in industries with slow growth." (https://www.investopedia.com/terms/e/ev-ebitda.asp)

multiple arbitrage: "Multiple arbitrage is based on increasing the valuation of a company purely through profiting from differences in the asset's price. Value created from multiple arbitrage is independent of making operational improvements or realizing synergies. Private equity firms use this practice to create immediate positive returns. By adding a smaller company to a larger company, its valuation increases, and the business will trade at a higher multiple. Generally, multiple arbitrage takes advantage of price differences between two or more markets." (https://privateequitycxo.com/blog_posts/multiple-arbitrage-in-private-equity)

multiple on invested capital: "Multiple on Invested Capital ("MOIC") is a metric used to describe the value or performance of an investment relative to its initial cost, commonly used within private markets. MOIC is among the most relevant metrics to be assessed while conducting fund due diligence. It is also often referred to as Equity Multiple." (https://www.moonfare.com/glossary/multiple-on-invested-capital-moic)

objectives and key results (OKR): OKRs are a goal-setting tool for communicating what you want to accomplish and how to measure progress. (https://www.whatmatters.com/faqs/okr-meaning-definition-example)

organic growth: The typical actions most business owners use to grow their business "one customer at a time," with focus (often exclusively) on raising revenue and improving margins (keeping or getting costs low).

PE-backed strategic sale: "…It means there is a private equity puppeteer out there calling the shots for the company that is acquiring you. In that situation, you are then a bolt-on acquisition."

platform: "…the initial acquisition made by a Private Equity Group… The acquisition acts as the starting point for other acquisitions in the same industry." (https://corporatefinanceinstitute.com/resources/valuation/platform-company/)

private equity: "Private equity describes investment partnerships that buy and manage companies before selling them." (https://www.investopedia.com/terms/p/privateequity.asp)

private equity firm: "An equity firm or *private equity firm* refers to an investment company that utilizes its own funds or capital from other investors for its expansion and startup operations. Equity firms are usually not listed publicly, and their shares are not traded in the stock market. For this reason, equity firms are not subject to a majority of the regulations that public companies need to comply with. Often referred to as a financial sponsor, the firm will raise capital to invest according to specific investment strategies." (https://corporatefinanceinstitute.com/resources/career/equity-firm/)

quality of earnings (Q of E): "A company's quality of earnings is revealed by dismissing any anomalies, accounting tricks, or one-time events that may skew the real bottom-line numbers on performance… For example, during periods of high inflation, quality of earnings is considered poor for many or most companies. Their sales figures are inflated, too." (https://www.investopedia.com/terms/q/qualityofearnings.asp)

re-trade: A re-trade occurs when the potential buyer of a company reduces the amount of their original offer… and it will cost the seller heavily to back out of the transaction. … A re-trade can be seen as a form of power play on the part of the buyer... Re-trades can also happen for legitimate reasons ... During the due diligence process, the buyer may discover a flaw or shortcoming in the business being sold and thus lower its bid accordingly. (https://www.divestopedia.com/definition/6745/re-trade/)

rollup: "... is simply a growth strategy where a private equity firm, venture capital group or corporate venture fund invests in consolidating two or more companies. The roll-up operator then works to streamline operations, reduce duplicative costs and implement best practices across each business." (https://www.forbes.com/sites/forbesfinancecouncil/2023/11/16/the-power-of-a-roll-up-growth-strategy/)

scrum: "... think of Scrum as a way to get work done as a team in small pieces at a time, with continuous experimentation and feedback loops along the way to learn and improve as you go. Scrum helps people and teams deliver value incrementally in a collaborative way." (https://search.brave.com/search?q=scrum&source=desktop)

software-as-a-service (SaaS): "... software ... used to manage and automate the process of subscribing to and using software-as-a-service (SaaS)..." (https://www.apptension.com/blog-posts/saas-subscription-solutions)

standard operating procedure: Standard operating procedures provide the policies, processes and standards needed for the organization to succeed. They can benefit a business by reducing errors, increasing efficiencies and profitability, creating a safe work environment and producing guidelines for how to resolve issues and overcome obstacles. (https://www.techtarget.com/searchbusinessanalytics/definition/standard-operating-procedure-SOP)

strategic buyer: "... a company or investor that seeks to acquire companies or assets, whose acquisition will add synergistic value to their existing portfolio. Strategic buyers are often in the same industry as the target companies, but not always." (https://www.linkedin.com/pulse/strategic-buyer-definition-benefits-comparison-examples-kison-patel)

strategic growth: The strategies private equity is known for employing expertly for accelerated growth of a business, including management of capital, acquisitions, and raising the industry multiple as it applies to their business.

strategic sale: "Strategic Sale means any, or combination of, (a) a transaction that leads to any change of Control (including sale of more than 50% (fifty percent) of the Company's Shares and other securities to any third party); or (b) an amalgamation or merger or acquisition of the Company with or by, as the case maybe, with another company resulting in a change in Control, or (c) sale of all or substantially all of the Assets of the Company. (https://www.lawinsider.com/dictionary/strategic-sale)

sweating the assets: "… the better utilisation of structures that are already in place and spending low extra or marginal costs in order to exploit better what's been built and spent already." (https://sharkfinesse.com/financial-terms/sweating-the-assets)

total addressable market (TAM): Total Addressable Market (TAM), also referred to as total available market, is a way for companies to determine how much money they could make if they sold their product or service to every possible customer in a specific market. TAM helps businesses understand the maximum revenue they could generate if they had 100% market share. For example, say a company produces organic energy bars. Its TAM would be the total potential revenue it could generate by selling its products to everyone interested in buying organic energy bars. (https://www.semrush.com/blog/total-addressable-market/)

vertical expansion: "… is when a company moves to perform a service or produce a good on a few different parts of the supply chain." (https://study.com/academy/lesson/vertical-expansion-in-business-definition-examples.html)

vintage: "… the first year a fund makes an investment, so as to factor in common economic and other factors they have performed under."

vivid vision: A Vivid Vision is far more precise that a traditional vision or mission statement, and it's more than just a number. It's not just about getting your business to a value of, say, $30 million. It's about envisioning what the company is like at that point. What's the culture? What sort of people are on board? What kinds of customers are you working with? (See *Vivid Vision: A Remarkable Tool For Aligning Your Business Around a Shared Vision of the Future* by Cameron Herold — https://www.amazon.com/Vivid-Vision-Remarkable-Aligning-Business-ebook/dp/B079XWZYHG/)

Notes

[1] Private equity describes investment partnerships that buy and manage companies before selling them. —https://www.investopedia.com/terms/p/privateequity.asp

[2] https://www.forbes.com/sites/kevinkruse/2012/11/28/zig-ziglar-10-quotes-that-can-change-your-life/?sh=68744e8e26a0

[3] Legendary motivational speaker and business consultant Zig Ziglar died yesterday, after a 40-year speaking career that saw him travel more than five million miles, consult for Fortune 500 companies and consort with American presidents and other world leaders. —https://www.entrepreneur.com/leadership/zig-ziglar-a-life-lived-at-the-top/225115

[4] "9,900 GP (General Partner) profiles" —https://www.privateequityinternational.com/private-equity-data/

[5] The private equity industry has grown rapidly over time. In 2021, private equity buyouts totalled a record $1.1 trillion, doubling from 2020. The industry is the most popular when stock prices are high and investment costs are low. In 2020, there were approximately 4,500 private equity firms in the U.S. with 16,000 private equity-backed companies. When combining private equity, hedge funds and investment vehicle businesses, there are 14,089 businesses in 2023. This is a 2.4% increase from 2022. California, Texas and New York have the highest number of private equity firms. —https://stachecow.com/how-many-private-equity-firms-are-in-the-us-193#stories

[6] An equity firm or private equity *firm* refers to an investment company that utilizes its own funds or capital from other investors for its expansion and startup operations. Equity firms are usually not listed publicly, and their shares are not traded in the stock market. For this reason, equity firms are not subject to a majority of the regulations that public companies need to comply with. Often referred to as a financial sponsor, the firm will raise capital to invest according to specific investment strategies. —
https://corporatefinanceinstitute.com/resources/career/equity-firm/

[7] Getty Images Holdings, Inc. operates as a creator and distributor of award-winning still imagery, video, music, and multimedia products. The company provides other forms of premium digital content, including music. Its award-winning photographers and imagery help customers produce inspiring work which appears every day in the world's most influential newspapers, magazines, advertising campaigns, films, television programs, and books. The company was formerly known as Getty Images, Inc. The company was founded in 1995 and is based in Seattle, Washington. —
https://finance.yahoo.com/quote/GETY/profile?p=GETY

[8] A roll-up is simply a growth strategy where a private equity firm, venture capital group or corporate venture fund invests in consolidating two or more companies. The roll-up operator then works to streamline operations, reduce duplicative costs and implement best practices across each business. —https://www.forbes.com/sites/forbesfinancecouncil/2023/11/16/the-power-of-a-roll-up-growth-strategy/

[9] Enterprise multiple... is a ratio used to determine the value of a company... Enterprise multiples can vary depending on the industry. Higher enterprise multiples are expected in high-growth industries and lower multiples in industries with slow growth. —
https://www.investopedia.com/terms/e/ev-ebitda.asp

[10] The average U.S. billionaire has overseen or been involved in more than 33 M&A transactions, having grown or sold their businesses. There are many reasons why M&A can be so successful for aspiring billionaires. First, it allows you to gain access to valuable resources and assets that you may not have been able to acquire on your own. Additionally, it often involves working with talented individuals who bring fresh perspectives and ideas to the table. And perhaps most importantly, M&A can give you the chance to scale your business much faster than if you were going it alone. So if you want to make it big someday, consider getting into mergers and acquisitions. —https://www.fool.com/the-ascent/personal-finance/articles/how-to-use-4-strategies-that-made-billionaires-rich/

[11] Billionaire Andrew Carnegie famously said that 90% of millionaires got their wealth by investing in real estate. We wanted to know: Is this still true? Is investing in real estate still a good idea? According to these nine Advisors in The Oracles, who made millions by investing in real estate, the answer is a resounding yes. —https://www.cnbc.com/2019/10/01/real-estate-is-still-the-best-investment-you-can-make-today-millionaires-say.html

[12] https://www.forbes.com/sites/jamesodonnell/2022/04/06/how-to-become-a-billionaire-these-industries-have-the-most-people-on-the-2022-forbes-list/?sh=5b3464c76898

[13] EBITDA, which stands for earnings before interest, taxes, depreciation, and amortization, is a metric used to measure a company's financial health and ability to generate cash flow. —https://www.businessnewsdaily.com/4461-ebitda-formula-definition.html

[14] A multiple or "multiplier" is applied to a specific financial metric of a company to calculate the business' valuation or assess its reasonability. The most common financial metrics that multiples are applied to include:

- EBITDA (earnings before interest, taxes, depreciation and amortization)
- EBIT (earnings before interest and depreciation)
- Net Earnings
- Revenue

If a multiple is applied to a pre-debt number, like EBITDA, EBIT or Revenue, the resulting valuation is the estimated enterprise value. If the multiple is applies to an after debt number, such as net earnings, the resulting valuation is the estimated equity value. A multiple is referred to as "4 times", "4x" or "4 turns", as an example, which would refer to EBITDA being multiplied times 4 to yield the estimated valuation of a company.
—https://www.divestopedia.com/definition/848/multiple/

[15] C-suite, or C-level, is widely-used vernacular describing the upper echelons of a corporation's senior executives and managers. C-suite gets its name from the titles of top senior executives, which tend to start with the letter C, for "chief," as in chief executive officer (CEO), chief financial officer (CFO), chief operating officer (COO), and chief information officer (CIO). —https://www.investopedia.com/terms/c/c-suite.asp

[16] For a long list of controversies, see https://en.wikipedia.org/wiki/Controversies_involving_Uber

[17] "WeWork, once valued at $47 billion, files for bankruptcy" —https://www.cnbc.com/2023/11/07/wework-files-for-bankruptcy.html

[18] "Enron Scandal: The Fall of a Wall Street Darling" —https://www.investopedia.com/updates/enron-scandal-summary/

[19] Churn rate, also known as attrition rate or customer churn, is the rate at which customers stop doing business with an entity.
—https://www.investopedia.com/terms/c/churnrate.asp

[20] https://www.azquotes.com/author/38572-Jay_Conrad_Levinson

---

[21] The customer lifetime value (LTV), also known as lifetime value, is the total revenue a company expects to earn over the lifetime of their relationship with a single customer. The customer lifetime value calculation accounts for the customer acquisition costs, operating expenses, and costs to produce the goods or services that the company is manufacturing. —https://corporatefinanceinstitute.com/resources/valuation/lifetime-value-calculation/

[22] Sweating the assets means the better utilisation of structures that are already in place and spending low extra or marginal costs in order to exploit better what's been built and spent already. —https://sharkfinesse.com/financial-terms/sweating-the-assets

[23] SaaS subscription management software is a type of software that is used to manage and automate the process of subscribing to and using software-as-a-service (SaaS) products... Such software allows them to manage their customers' subscriptions and usage, track revenue and usage trends, and provide a better customer experience. SaaS subscription management software is also highly beneficial for businesses that use multiple SaaS products, allowing them to manage all of their subscriptions in one place. —https://www.apptension.com/blog-posts/saas-subscription-solutions

[24] The long tail is a business strategy that allows companies to realize significant profits by selling low volumes of hard-to-find items to many customers, instead of only selling large volumes of a reduced number of popular items. The term was first coined in 2004 by Chris Anderson, who argued that products in low demand or with low sales volume can collectively make up market share that rivals or exceeds the relatively few current bestsellers and blockbusters but only if the store or distribution channel is large enough. —https://www.investopedia.com/terms/l/long-tail.asp

[25] https://medium.com/@robmoore_34140/systems-routines-habits-results-ca83a43585c3

[26] KPI stands for Key Performance Indicator, which is a quantifiable measure of performance over time for a specific objective. —https://www.qlik.com/us/kpi

[27] A company's quality of earnings is revealed by dismissing any anomalies, accounting tricks, or one-time events that may skew the real bottom-line numbers on performance. Once these are removed, the earnings that are derived from higher sales or lower costs can be seen clearly. Even factors external to the company can affect an evaluation of the quality of earnings. For example, during periods of high inflation, quality of earnings is considered poor for many or most companies. Their sales figures are inflated, too. —https://www.investopedia.com/terms/q/qualityofearnings.asp

[28] Fractional Finance exists to bring high growth start-ups together with a high calibre commercial CFO. This is typically the time when companies need senior, strategic leadership in the finance function to partner with the CEO, but the role does not yet warrant a full-time position. Initial areas of focus are typically cash flow, forecasting, strategy, fundraising, unit economics, decision-making frameworks, and getting the team on a clear path to scale. —https://fractionalfinance.co/

---

[29] A platform company refers to the initial acquisition made by a Private Equity Group in a specific industry or marketplace. The acquisition acts as the starting point for other acquisitions in the same industry. Platform companies create value by facilitating exchanges between consumers and producers of goods or services. For the exchanges to happen, the platform company creates large networks of users and resources that can be accessed on demand. —https://corporatefinanceinstitute.com/resources/valuation/platform-company/

[30] The buy and build strategy is when a company expands its operations by acquiring a platform company with developed expertise that it can then build out. When a business requires growth and expansion, there are several possibilities to consider. The company can develop its internal capabilities that will drive the expansion, or it can buy a business with an already developed expertise in that area of specialization and build it out further. The buy and build strategy adopts the latter option. The effect can create great value since the operations of several smaller firms combine to add value to the new firm. —
https://corporatefinanceinstitute.com/resources/management/buy-and-build-strategy/

[31] There are tiers in private equity. Think of it like a bell curve. The top of the bell curve, where there is the most activity, is generally what is called the "mid-market." The transactions in this mid-market run usually somewhere between $50 million and up to $300 million. Sometimes people say higher, but the sweet spot, if you like, of the mid-market private equity firms, is that range. The reason why I say $5 million EBITDA is if you can get to that and you sell your company for 10x or higher, you're going to be in the biggest part of the market, where there is the most capital that has not yet been deployed. It gets you playing in the lane of mid-market private equity, which is where the majority of capital sits currently. More on this later.

[32] See "rollup" on page 20.

[33] It's worth reading how Alexis Sikorsky explains this in his book *Cashing Out*, in particular check out pages 60-70.

[34] Assets under management (AUM) is the market value of the investments managed by a person or entity on behalf of clients. AUM is used in conjunction with management performance and management experience when evaluating a company. When calculating AUM, some financial institutions include bank deposits, mutual funds, and cash, while others limit it to funds under discretionary management from individual investors. —
https://www.investopedia.com/terms/a/aum.asp

[35] Private equity and venture capital funds usually are organized to have a limited life cycle, often in the range of 7 to 15 years. —
https://www.strictlybusinesslawblog.com/2017/06/29/the-life-cycle-of-a-private-equity-or-venture-capital-fund/

[36] When reading this section, please note that the PE *firm* and the PE *fund* are different things. One PE firm can have multiple funds at the same time, and any LP may invest in one or all of the funds, but each investment is separate and associated just with the fund the money is invested in.

[37] Remember, in Part One we introduced the term *multiple*, and an industry multiple is the ratio used to determine the value of a company. Multiples vary depending on the industry. Higher multiples are expected in high-growth industries and lower multiples in industries with slow growth. We'll discuss and compare a few industry multiples later in this book.

[38] A capital call, also known as a "draw down," is the act of collecting funds from limited partners whenever the need arises. When an investor buys into a private equity fund, the firm makes an agreement with the investor that these funds will be available when the firm requests them. In turn, investors are able to hold onto their funds and keep them in a favorable investment account, such as a mutual fund or retirement account, so that the investment can continue to appreciate until the firm needs it. — https://www.securedocs.com/blog/private-equity-what-is-a-capital-call

[39] The key thing to understand here is that each fund may buy on average 7-10 "platform" businesses (from the fund). The goal is to grow, scale, and exit these platforms (with bolt-on acquisitions, etc.) over a 3-7 year period. So even though the LP may commit to 10+ years of the fund's existence, they will be realising liquidity events earlier than this. They will also have a few investments end up in the toilet, but on aggregate, they expect +70% of those initial platforms to win.

[40] Distributions, the means by which private equity funds return capital to investors, are paid when fund managers realise their investments in underlying companies or assets. — https://www.moonfare.com/blog/private-equity-distributions

[41] Multiple arbitrage is based on increasing the valuation of a company purely through profiting from differences in the asset's price. Value created from multiple arbitrage is independent of making operational improvements or realizing synergies. Private equity firms use this practice to create immediate positive returns. By adding a smaller company to a larger company, its valuation increases, and the business will trade at a higher multiple. Generally, multiple arbitrage takes advantage of price differences between two or more markets. —https://privateequitycxo.com/blog_posts/multiple-arbitrage-in-private-equity

[42] Market capitalization shows how much a company is worth as determined by the total market value of all outstanding shares. To calculate a company's market cap, multiply the number of outstanding shares by the current market value of one share. — https://www.investopedia.com/terms/m/marketcapitalization.asp

[43] https://www.investopedia.com/investing/compound-annual-growth-rate-what-you-should-know/

[44] ibid

[45] The required rate of return (hurdle rate) is the minimum return that an investor is expecting to receive for their investment. Essentially, the required rate is the minimum acceptable compensation for the investment's level of risk. The required rate of return is a key concept in corporate finance and equity valuation. — https://corporatefinanceinstitute.com/resources/career-map/sell-side/capital-markets/required-rate-of-return/

---

[46] Carried interest, or 'carry' for short, is the percentage of a private fund's investment profits that a fund manager receives as compensation. Used primarily by private equity funds, including venture capital funds, carry is one of the primary ways fund managers are paid. — https://carta.com/learn/private-funds/management/carried-interest/

[47] These funds have a similar fee structure to that of hedge funds, typically consisting of a management fee (generally 2%) and a performance fee (usually 20%). — https://www.investopedia.com/articles/investing/072115/private-equity-management-fees-regulation.asp

[48] Capital markets are venues where savings and investments are channelled between suppliers and those in need of capital. — https://www.investopedia.com/terms/c/capitalmarkets.asp

[49] lever, noun. 1a: a bar used for prying or dislodging something, 1b: an inducing or compelling force : TOOL ("use food as a political lever"). Etymology (Noun and Verb) Middle English, from Anglo-French levier, lever, from lever to raise, from Latin levare, from levis light in weight —https://www.merriam-webster.com/dictionary/lever

[50] "Total Addressable Market (TAM), also referred to as total available market, is a way for companies to determine how much money they could make if they sold their product or service to every possible customer in a specific market. TAM helps businesses understand the maximum revenue they could generate if they had 100% market share. For example, say a company produces organic energy bars. Its TAM would be the total potential revenue it could generate by selling its products to everyone interested in buying organic energy bars." —And see the excellent article this comes from here: https://www.semrush.com/blog/total-addressable-market/

[51] "... we often refer to high-end clients as "champagne" clients and they are defined by these 3 criteria: (1) What makes them a champagne client is that you love working with them, they are up to great work in the world and you know you can help them make some significant changes. (2) They are long-term clients – they understand that the real work of creating significant change and fabulous results does not happen overnight and they value working with you for a year or more. (3) They are willing to invest more time, energy and money to achieve the long-term changes they are seeking." — https://businessgrowthacademy.com/is-your-business-filled-with-champagne-clients/

[52] Throughout this book we do discuss real-life examples of exits I have been involved in, and these normally require strict confidentiality and have NDAs in place.

[53] Sometimes "keeping costs low" is not a good strategy. It's not simply cutting costs as much as having the right costs that will support revenue and profitability. It's about being intelligent with how you look at your costs, about being disciplined around it.

[54] See *Vivid Vision: A Remarkable Tool For Aligning Your Business Around a Shared Vision of the Future* by Cameron Herold — https://www.amazon.com/Vivid-Vision-Remarkable-Aligning-Business-ebook/dp/B079XWZYHG/

---

[55] https://cameronherold.com/vivid-vision/

[56] strategic buyer: "… a company or investor that seeks to acquire companies or assets, whose acquisition will add synergistic value to their existing portfolio. Strategic buyers are often in the same industry as the target companies, but not always." — https://www.linkedin.com/pulse/strategic-buyer-definition-benefits-comparison-examples-kison-patel

[57] financial buyer: "… long-term investors interested in the return that they can get by buying a well-managed company. Financial buyers look to generate cash flow by boosting revenue, cutting costs, or creating economies of scale by buying similar companies." — https://www.investopedia.com/terms/f/financial-buyer.asp

[58] See Part One

[59] https://www.investopedia.com/terms/e/ev-ebitda.asp

[60] Shadow accounting is the practice of keeping a second set of financial records to verify information in the primary books or to make management decisions that are not supported by the general ledger. —https://www.allvuesystems.com/resources/what-is-shadow-accounting-and-why-do-private-equity-funds-do-it/

[61] Standard operating procedures provide the policies, processes and standards needed for the organization to succeed. They can benefit a business by reducing errors, increasing efficiencies and profitability, creating a safe work environment and producing guidelines for how to resolve issues and overcome obstacles. — https://www.techtarget.com/searchbusinessanalytics/definition/standard-operating-procedure-SOP

[62] *Talent-to-Value* is a concept I got from Sandy Ogg. See www.CEOWorks.com.

[63] In soccer and some other team sports, a striker is a player who mainly attacks and scores goals, rather than defends. — https://www.collinsdictionary.com/us/dictionary/english/striker

[64] "OKR" stands for "Objectives and Key Results." OKRs are a goal-setting tool for communicating what you want to accomplish and how to measure progress. — https://www.whatmatters.com/faqs/okr-meaning-definition-example

[65] ...think of Scrum as a way to get work done as a team in small pieces at a time, with continuous experimentation and feedback loops along the way to learn and improve as you go. Scrum helps people and teams deliver value incrementally in a collaborative way. — https://search.brave.com/search?q=scrum&source=desktop

[66] https://pixabay.com/vectors/archimedes-lever-quarryman-worker-148273/

[67] https://hf.com/portfolio/getty-images-inc/

---

[68] Value attribution bias refers to the tendency to overestimate the value or quality of an item, person, or decision based solely on our perception of its worth or status. —https://www.growthink.com/content/how-value-attribution-can-dramatically-help-or-hurt-your-chances-raising-money

[69] A fractional CFO is an experienced finance professional who provides services for organizations in a part-time, retainer, or contract arrangement. They offer a company the experience and expertise of a high-end CFO without the in-house cost of a full-time hire. —https://preferredcfo.com/what-is-fractional-cfo/

[70] An add back is an expense that will not be included in the buyer's future P&Ls for the company. Understanding and applying add backs and other kinds of adjustments helps normalize a business's earnings on a go-forward basis. This will give all parties a true understanding of the cash flow, and therefore, the true value of the company. —https://melcap.com/understanding-add-backs-selling-business/

[71] In management buy-in, a company is purchased by a manager or a management team from outside the company. The target company is acquired by these outside investors when they feel that the company is underperforming and its products can generate greater than current yields with the change in current business strategy and/or management. —https://efinancemanagement.com/mergers-and-acquisitions/management-buy-in

[72] An ESOP is an employee benefit plan that enables employees to own part or all of the company they work for. ESOPs are most commonly used to facilitate succession planning, allowing a company owner to sell his or her shares and transition flexibly out of the business... ESOPs can create higher productivity, employee retention, tax advantages and higher job satisfaction. ESOPs are also attractive because they provide a financing tool for the company, who can sell its stock to the ESOP and use the cash to pay off debt, etc. —https://www.wcl.american.edu/academics/experientialedu/clinical/theclinics/elc/tlcc/for-businesses-nonprofits/esops-info-sheet/#:~:text=An%20ESOP%20is%20an%20employee,flexibly%20out%20of%20the%20business.

[73] Growth equity funds target companies that have potential for scalable and renewed growth. Unlike buyout funds, they usually take a minority stake with the intention of growing the business as much as possible. But - like buyout funds - the goal is to exit at a higher multiple. —https://www.moonfare.com/pe-masterclass/growth-equity

[74] ... family offices have greater control. They can choose how much they want to get involved in the business and plan their existing strategies. And since it avoids the fee requirements associated with private equity funds, it could lead to higher returns. —https://andsimple.co/insights/family-offices-investing-in-private-equity/

[75] Wealthy people often are divided into two categories, high-net-worth individuals (HNWIS) who have at least $1 million in liquid assets and ultra-high-net-worth individuals (UHNWIS) with $30 million and up. —https://smartasset.com/investing/high-net-worth-vs-ultra-high-net-worth

---

[76] Trailing 12 months (TTM) is a term that describes the past 12 consecutive months of a company's performance data used for reporting financial figures. These figures represent a more current picture of a business's financial performance than using its annual filings and reports, which, at times, can contain information that is nearly one year old. —https://www.investopedia.com/terms/t/ttm.asp

[77] Revenue run rate (also called annual run rate or sales run rate) is a method of projecting upcoming revenue over a longer time period (usually one year) based on previously earned revenue. For example, if your business reported $15,000 in sales in the last quarter, your annual run rate would be $60,000. —https://www.paddle.com/resources/revenue-run-rate

[78] An earnout is a contractual provision stating that the seller of a business is to obtain additional compensation in the future if the business achieves certain financial goals, which are usually stated as a percentage of gross sales or earnings. —https://www.investopedia.com/terms/e/earnout.asp

[79] A data room is a secure space where confidential documents can be kept and only read by people authorized to access them. When businesses need a secure location to share confidential documents with selected third parties, they use a data room to control who gets to see what. This minimizes risk that their confidential business information will be exposed to unauthorized parties. Traditionally, data room due diligence was conducted in a physical room. Today, it happens online in what are called virtual data rooms. —https://www.ansarada.com/what-is-data-room

www.ingramcontent.com/pod-product-compliance
Ingram Content Group UK Ltd.
Pitfield, Milton Keynes, MK11 3LW, UK
UKHW020033121026
15625UKWH00061B/747/J

9 781068 243905